Drug Therapy and Adjustment Disorders

Psychiatric Disorders
Drugs and Psychology for the Mind and Body

Drug Therapy and Adjustment Disorders

Drug Therapy and Anxiety Disorders

Drug Therapy and Cognitive Disorders

Drug Therapy and Childhood and Adolescent Disorders

Drug Therapy and Dissociative Disorders

Drug Therapy and Eating Disorders

Drug Therapy and Impulse Control Disorders

Drug Therapy for Mental Disorders Caused by a Medical Condition

Drug Therapy and Mood Disorders

Drug Therapy and Obsessive-Compulsive Disorder

Drug Therapy and Personality Disorders

Drug Therapy and Postpartum Disorders

Drug Therapy and Premenstrual Disorders

Drug Therapy and Psychosomatic Disorders

Drug Therapy and Schizophrenia

Drug Therapy and Sexual Disorders

Drug Therapy and Sleep Disorders

Drug Therapy and Substance-Related Disorders

The FDA and Psychiatric Drugs: How a Drug Is Approved

Psychiatric Disorders: Drugs and Psychology for the Mind and Body

Drug Therapy and Adjustment Disorders

BY SHERRY BONNICE

MASON CREST PUBLISHERS

PHILADELPHIA

Mason Crest Publishers Inc.
370 Reed Road, Broomall, Pennsylvania 19008
(866) MCP-BOOK (toll free)
www.masoncrest.com

First Edition, 2004
13 12 11 10 09 08 07 06   10 9 8 7 6 5 4 3 2

Bonnice, Sherry, 1956–
Drug therapy for adjustment disorders / by Sherry Bonnice.
v. cm.—(Psychiatric disorders: drugs and psychology for the mind and body)
Includes bibliographical references and index.
        ISBN 1-59084-560-9
        ISBN 1-59084-559-5 (series)
Contents: What is an adjustment disorder?—History of psychiatric drugs—How do
the drugs work?—Treatment description—Case studies—Risks and side effects of
drug therapy—Alternative and supplementary treatments.
1. Adjustment disorders—Juvenile literature. 2. Adjustment disorders—
Chemotherapy—Juvenile literature. 3. Adjustment disorders—Treatment—Juvenile
literature. [1. Adjustment disorders. 2. Mental health.] I. Title. II. Series.
RC455.4.S87B66 2004
618.92'89'18—dc21
        2003004853

Produced by Harding House Publishing Service
www.hardinghousepages.com
Composition by Bytheway Publishing Services, Binghamton, New York.
Cover design by Benjamin Stewart.
Printed in the Hashemite Kingdom of Jordan.

This book is meant to educate and should not be used as an
alternative to appropriate medical care. Its creators have made
every effort to ensure that the information presented is
accurate—but it is not intended to substitute for the help and
services of trained professionals.

CONTENTS

INTRODUCTION

by Mary Ann Johnson

Teenagers have reason to be interested in psychiatric disorders and their treatment. Friends, family members, and even teens themselves may experience one of these disorders. Using scenarios adolescents will understand, this series explains various psychiatric disorders and the drugs that treat them.

Diagnosis and treatment of psychiatric disorders in children between six and eighteen years old are well studied and documented in the scientific journals. In 1998, Roberts and colleagues identified and reviewed fifty-two research studies that attempted to identify the overall prevalence of child and adolescent psychiatric disorders Estimates of prevalence in this review ranged from one percent to nearly 51 percent. Various other studies have reported similar findings. Needless to say, many children and adolescents are suffering from psychiatric disorders and are in need of treatment.

Many children have more than one psychiatric disorder, which complicates their diagnoses and treatment plans. Psychiatric disorders often occur together. For instance, a person with a sleep disorder may also be depressed; a teenager with attention-deficit/hyperactivity disorder (ADHD) may also have a substance-use disorder. In psychiatry, we call this comorbidity. Much research addressing this issue has led to improved diagnosis and treatment.

The most common child and adolescent psychiatric disorders are anxiety disorders, depressive disorders, and ADHD. Sleep disorders, sexual disorders, eating disorders, substance-abuse disorders, and psychotic disorders are also quite common. This series has volumes that address each of these disorders.

Major depressive disorders have been the most commonly diagnosed mood disorders for children and adolescents. Researchers don't agree as to how common mania and bipolar disorder are in children. Some experts believe that manic episodes in children and adolescents are underdiagnosed. Many times, a mood disturbance may occur with another psychiatric disorder. For instance, children with ADHD may also be depressed. ADHD is just one psychiatric disorder that is a major health concern for children, adolescents, and adults. Studies of ADHD have reported prevalence rates among children that range from two to 12 percent.

Failure to understand or seek treatment for psychiatric disorders puts children and young adults at risk of developing substance-use disorders. For example, recent research indicates that those with ADHD who were treated with medication were 85 percent less likely to develop a substance-use disorder. Results like these emphasize the importance of timely diagnosis and treatment.

Early diagnosis and treatment may prevent these children from developing further psychological problems. Books like those in this series provide important information, a vital first step toward increased awareness of psychological disorders; knowledge and understanding can shed light on even the most difficult subject. These books should never, however, be viewed as a substitute for professional consultation. Psychiatric testing and an evaluation by a licensed professional is recommended to determine the needs of the child or adolescent and to establish an appropriate treatment plan.

FOREWORD

by Donald Esherick

We live in a society filled with technology—from computers surfing the Internet to automobiles operating on gas and batteries. In the midst of this advanced society, diseases, illnesses, and medical conditions are treated and often cured with the administration of drugs, many of which were unknown thirty years ago. In the United States, we are fortunate to have an agency, the Food and Drug Administration (FDA), which monitors the development of new drugs and then determines whether the new drugs are safe and effective for use in human beings.

When a new drug is developed, a pharmaceutical company usually intends that drug to treat a single disease or family of diseases. The FDA reviews the company's research to determine if the drug is safe for use in the population at large and if it effectively treats the targeted illnesses. When the FDA finds that the drug is safe and effective, it approves the drug for treating that specific disease or condition. This is called the labeled indication.

During the routine use of the drug, the pharmaceutical company and physicians often observe that a drug treats other medical conditions besides what is indicated in the labeling. While the labeling will not include the treatment of the particular condition, a physician can still prescribe the drug to a patient with this disease. This is known as an unlabeled or off-label indication. This series contains information about both the labeled and off-label indications of psychiatric drugs.

I have reviewed the books in this series from the perspective of the pharmaceutical industry and the FDA, specifically focusing on the labeled indications, uses, and known side effects of these drugs. Further information can be found on the FDA's Web page (www.FDA.gov).

Marital tension can cause problems for the entire family. Children may have difficulty adjusting to the constant stress.

1 | What Is an Adjustment Disorder?

Gabe felt anxious and couldn't concentrate on his teacher's lecture. As he sat at his desk, he squeezed and twisted his hands, almost as if to keep them warm. His thoughts went back to the argument his parents had had the night before. Gabe could still hear the shouting and then the final, "I'll leave and then we'll both be happier," and the reply, "Great, that will be best for everyone." His mom ran upstairs as his dad stepped quietly into the family room.

Gabe knew his family had been having trouble. In fact, he had felt terrible most of the time lately. His parents fought every time they were together, and his little brother cried himself to sleep most nights. What had started all this fighting? Why couldn't he think of something to do, something to make his parents stop and be like they used to be? Didn't they see what this was doing to him and his brother?

He held his head. When would this headache go away? He would have to go to the nurse again today. He just couldn't stand it anymore. *I wonder what she will ask today.* He wasn't going to tell her the reason for his headache. He couldn't stand the thought of his dad moving out, but he wasn't going to tell the nurse that. He had to make a plan and do something soon. But in the meantime, he felt as though he couldn't cope with life anymore.

The definition for *adjustment* in the dictionary says that it is "the act of bringing to a more satisfactory state, to settle or resolve." It also says "to adapt or conform oneself to new conditions, or to achieve mental and behavioral balance between one's own needs and the demands of others." Gabe felt out of balance because of the difficulties his parents

Adjustment has to do with achieving a satisfactory balance between opposing life factors. When the various elements of a life are weighed, this balance is often difficult to achieve.

Subtypes of Adjustment Disorders

Adjustment disorder with depressed moods may display symptoms of depressed moods, tearfulness, or feelings of hopelessness.

Adjustment disorder with anxiety may display symptoms of nervousness, worry, jitteriness, or fear of separation from major attachment figures.

Adjustment disorder with anxiety and depressed moods may display a combination of symptoms from both of the previous subtypes (depressed moods and anxiety).

Adjustment disorder with disturbance of conduct may display symptoms of improper behavior toward others or violation of societal norms and rules (truancy, destruction of property, reckless driving, fighting, etc.).

Adjustment disorder with mixed disturbance of emotions and conduct may display a combination of symptoms from all of the previous subtypes (depressed moods, anxiety, and conduct).

Adjustment disorder unspecified may display reactions to stressful events that do not fit in one of the previous subtypes. Reactions may include behaviors such as social withdrawal or inhibitions to normally expected activities (for example, school or work).

---

were having. Only a few months before, his parents' arguments seemed under control. They argued, but they also made up and things went back to normal within a day or two. However, in the last couple of months, every argument ended with his dad sleeping in the family room and one of his parents saying the only solution was separation.

However, Gabe's problem is more than just the worry about his parents' possible separation; he is suffering from real physical and mental symptoms that get worse each day. He has been jumpy and withdrawn from the other kids. He doesn't hang out with his friends after school and spends a lot of time with his younger brother. He can't get his parents out of his mind, and all the thinking gives him a constant

headache. He doesn't want to spend time with one or the other of his parents; he doesn't want to have to move; he doesn't want one of them to move. He just wants things resolved—but he can't make that happen. Family discord is a part of his reality; but Gabe can't cope with that reality. He may be suffering from an adjustment disorder.

An adjustment disorder is an emotional or behavioral reaction to a specific and identifiable stressful event. This reaction is not considered an expected response. Instead, the person seems to be suffering more than is normal for his age and circumstances. Adjustment disorders are usually the result of short-term upheavals. In general, the event is a normal life experience, such as losing a job, breaking off a relationship, moving to another community or school—or family problems. The beginning of the disorder is usually

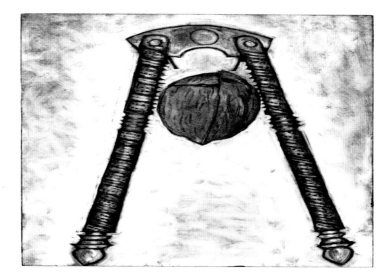

Life's stressors may feel like an emotional nutcracker, squeezing tighter and tighter until something breaks.

within three months of the disturbing event, but could occur almost immediately.

Adults usually develop adjustment disorders because of problems in their marriages, work, or finances. Adolescents' stressors might include problems with understanding certain subjects or other school-related disturbances, rejection from parents or friends, or their parents' marital problems. How a person reacts to the stressors is often related to factors such as economic conditions and available support systems. Most of the time the *stressor* is a specific experience that causes great stress, change, or disappointment in the person's life—such as a missed job promotion, as was the case in Pat's life.

GLOSSARY

stressor: A stimulus that causes physical or mental tension.

Pat felt he was the only person qualified to be promoted as sales manager for his company—but suddenly, a nephew of the owner appeared at work, and within two weeks this newcomer had that position. Pat began to feel nervous and jumpy all of the time. Normally, his head barely hit the pillow before he was asleep, but now he could no longer sleep well. This one-time event has caused Pat to experience an adjustment disorder.

Sometimes, however, the event can be recurring. For example, a job after school is a necessity for Missy. Her dad left the family when she was two, and her mom works hard to support her and her two brothers. However, there never seems to be enough money at the end of each month. Missy has to pay for all her clothes and many times for her lunch and any other costs for school functions. Unfortunately, her job at the grocery store always seems to be the busiest when she is working the hardest at school. Thanksgiving and Christmas are always so busy at school with concerts and finals. At the same time, work is also busy because of holiday entertaining and special dinners. Missy has to work longer hours, she gets little sleep, and by the time the holiday actu-

Hurricanes, floods, and other natural disasters are stressors that affect entire communities. Each individual will react differently, however, to the same event.

ally arrives, she is always sick. She too is experiencing an adjustment disorder.

Occasionally, an entire community may be affected by a natural disaster, such as a flood. Although one stressor has affected an entire group of people, each person will react according to her own set of circumstances. For instance, Bill and his family may cope easily with the hard work of cleaning up after a flood; they receive plenty of support that helps them keep the event in perspective. No one was hurt, and the possessions they treasured most, such as old pictures, were stored out of the flooded area of the house. Each night, Bill's family goes home to a hot meal at his parents' house. His parents live in a dry area only fifteen minutes from Bill's home, and his brother's family helps with the cleanup. His teenage children continue to see their friends, and the family finds many good times even in the midst of the cleanup work. Don, on the other hand, does not share the same experience. He is a single parent living far from any family. After the flood, he stayed with friends for a few nights, but they lived too far away and he had to miss work. He can't afford to do that for more than a few days, because he has only a few sick days and vacation time accumulated; the money for bills, child care, and food has been tight. Now he will have the additional expense of a place to stay and replacing needed things. Don snaps at his children for little things; then he feels guilty and out of control. He stays up late and gets up early to clean up the flood damage to his house, hoping his family can move back in as soon as possible—but his babysitter has said she can only work such long hours for a few more days. Don has experienced a great change and adjusting to it is difficult for him.

Disasters like those experienced by Don and Bill are common causes of adjustment disorders. Other sources of stress might be personal or employment relationships, financial issues, menopause, retirement, or illness. They may also include events such as robbery, miscarriage, tornadoes or earthquakes, being diagnosed with a *chronic* illness, or learning of a loved one's illness. Whatever the experience, those who live through it suffer a change that causes confusion and a feeling of crisis.

Everyone must live through many changes and transitions as a part of life. Experts believe that adjustment disorders are common, but because of their short-lived duration, not everyone gets help from a physician or a psychologist.

One of the key points in recognizing an adjustment disorder is the fact that the person suffers symptoms more severe than the stressor indicates. In other words, a person's reaction to the event is out of proportion to the expected reaction that most people would have to the same event. A diagnosis may be made by psychological evaluation, relating the symptoms to the time of the stressor, rating the symptoms as more severe than the stressor indicates, and determining that there are no other underlying disorders.

GLOSSARY

chronic: Something that is long-term and/or recurring.

The DSM-IV Definition of an Adjustment Disorder

Criterion A
The development of emotional or behavioral symptoms in response to an identifiable stressor(s) occurring within three months of the onset of the stressor(s).

Criterion B
The symptoms are in excess of what would be expected from exposure to the stressor or cause significant impairment in social or occupational (academic) functioning.

Criterion C
The stress-related disturbance does not meet the criteria for another specific Axis I disorder and is not merely an exacerbation of a preexisting Axis I or Axis II disorder.

Criterion D
The symptoms do not represent bereavement.
Once the stressor (or its consequences) has terminated, the disorder should resolve, usually within six months of termination of the stressor.

The symptoms of this disorder are similar to those of anxiety and depression; two of the disorder's subtypes include adjustment disorder with depressed moods or with anxiety. However, these symptoms can be present without a diagnosis of anxiety or depression. Some specific symptoms of adjustment disorder include irritability; tension; difficulty sleeping; feelings of fear, rage, hopelessness, or guilt; crying; excessive worry; and fears of separation from a primary attachment figure. Adjustment disorder usually disappears within six months of the termination or removal of the stressor.

Adjustment disorder can be either acute or chronic. Acute adjustment disorder indicates that the symptoms have been present for less than six months after the stressor

When life pulls at us from opposing directions, we may feel like a rope about to snap!

or its consequences have been resolved. A chronic specifier indicates that the symptoms have persisted for longer than six months. This can happen due to a chronic or disabling medical condition, such as hearing loss or diabetes, or a stressor with long-term consequences, such as major financial setbacks or divorce.

As with all psychiatric disorders, adjustment disorders affect the lives of more than just the patient. The person suffering from adjustment disorder has to cope with a great deal, of course, but so do the people with whom he comes into contact on a regular basis. A person experiencing an adjustment disorder often violates the rights of others: she may pay no attention to age-appropriate social norms, or he may break societal rules. Symptoms might include reckless driving, fighting, skipping school, underage smoking or drinking, and vandalism. Persons in authority need to be aware of what is happening in the lives of adolescents in

People sometimes dismiss adolescent behaviors that may actually be symptoms of an adjustment disorder.

order to recognize a possible adjustment disorder. It is often easy to excuse inappropriate behavior by believing that it is "just a phase" that all teenagers go through. However, this behavior may indicate that a young person is suffering and needs help.

Some people may know exactly why they feel a certain way, as Gabe does, but others may feel anxious and fearful, even depressed, and not know why. If the sufferer does not receive help in figuring out what has caused the stress, she could become clinically depressed or begin to suffer from anxiety that may last for years.

If a person is suspected of having an adjustment disorder, a thorough physical exam and mental evaluation are necessary in order to rule out any other serious physical or mental disorders. Diagnosis is the important first step on the road toward help and treatment.

When life's circumstances are no longer the same, we may have difficulty coping emotionally with the changes.

2 | History of Psychiatric Drugs

Amber's dad left at the end of the summer for a year-long overseas position working in the Army Reserve. She knew the importance of her dad's work, but she missed him, and when she saw her mom doing everyday activities as if everything was the same, she felt angry. Amber had a hard time falling asleep in the house without her dad; after all, she had been used to having him around for sixteen years. When he was not at the dinner table or at any of her basketball games, Amber felt like crying. Amber missed their Saturday-morning breakfast outings and the special times they spent together.

Often, Amber found herself snapping at her younger brother and sister. She spent a lot of time in her room and was always tired. At night, she tossed and turned and woke in the morning feeling as tired as she had the night before. After one of her teachers called her mother because of a failed test grade (not to mention Amber's surly attitude in class), her mother and the teacher decided to meet to discuss the problem. After some discussion, they both agreed Amber's difficulties were due to her father's absence.

Amber's mom wanted to help her cope with the change in her life. She decided to take her daughter to their family physician, and after examining Amber, the doctor felt she was suffering from adjustment disorder. Neither Amber nor her mother had ever heard of this illness, but as the doctor explained the symptoms and causes, they agreed that this might be her problem. The physician prescribed a mild antidepressant and a sleeping aid. She felt that once Amber started sleeping better she would be better able to adjust to her situation. The doctor also suggested that Amber talk to a counselor to help her voice her feelings and better understand what she was feeling.

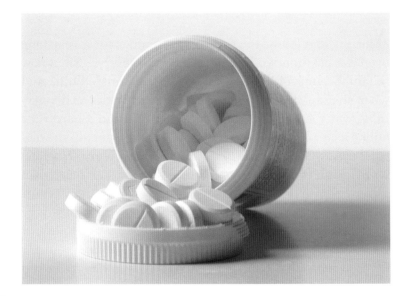

Antidepressant medications and sleeping aids may help relieve the symptoms of an adjustment disorder.

Drug Approval

Before a drug can be marketed in the United States, it must be officially approved by the Food and Drug Administration (FDA). Today's FDA is the primary consumer protection agency in the United States. Operating under the authority given it by the government, and guided by laws established throughout the twentieth century, the FDA has established a rigorous drug approval process that verifies the safety, effectiveness, and accuracy of labeling for any drug marketed in the United States.

While the United States has the FDA for the approval and regulation of drugs and medical devices, Canada has a similar organization called the Therapeutic Product Directorate (TPD). The TPD is a division of Health Canada, the Canadian government department of health. The TPD regulates drugs, medical devices, disinfectants, and sanitizers with disinfectant claims. Some of the things that the TPD monitors are quality, effectiveness, and safety. Just as the FDA must approve new drugs in the United States, the TPD must approve new drugs in Canada before those drugs can enter the market.

Throughout history, medications have been used to help alleviate the symptoms of disease. However, it has not been until recently that researchers have been able to create substances that are so specific as to affect only certain transmitters in the brain. This ability has made treating patients much more effective and much less damaging to other parts of the body. This allows physicians to help those persons who suffer from both a physical and a psychological disorder deal with them simultaneously.

HELP FROM ANTIDEPRESSANTS

Although antidepressants have been most widely used in the treatment of chronic psychiatric disorders, they have

been found to work in the treatment of short-term problems, such as adjustment disorder, as well. By altering the brain chemistry in depressed-adjustment disorder and allowing better sleep patterns for other types of adjustment disorders, the drug can help individuals better cope with the issues bothering them.

Antidepressants affect the way the brain functions as it sends messages throughout the nervous system from ***neuron*** to neuron. The small gap between each neuron is called a synapse; messages move across these gaps by way of chemicals called neurotransmitters. Once their job of relaying the message is accomplished, the neurotransmitters are partially broken down and sent as waste to the kidneys. The remaining neurotransmitters are reabsorbed back into the nerve by a process called reuptake. By forcing the neurotransmitter to remain in the synapse longer, the brain has more neurotransmitter at its disposal as it sends messages. To accomplish this, reuptake needs to be partially inhibited.

Antidepressants known as selective serotonin reuptake inhibitors (SSRIs) cause only the neurotransmitter serotonin to be inhibited from the reuptake phase. Serotonin also affects mood and therefore emotion. Antidepressants, such as Zoloft and Prozac, are from the SSRI group. They change the brain's chemistry by keeping serotonin from being reabsorbed within the brain. By making sure that more serotonin is available within the brain, the deficiency is eliminated and so are many of the psychiatric symptoms.

The SSRIs are a relatively new antidepressant. Their discovery is the result of research that began with one of the first antidepressants, iproniazid phosphate. Originally studied and used to treat tuberculosis in the early 1950s, physicians noticed that the patients who took this drug became more energetic and elevated in mood, even though their tuberculosis was not improving. These happier patients led

Some of the antidepressants that were developed before SSRIs caused bizarre mood elevation. These drugs overstimulated the brain.

researchers to evaluate the drug more carefully to find out if it had any effect on those suffering from depression.

Treating depressed patients with iproniazid became prevalent after a 1957 article was published, stating that research showed its success in improving the symptoms of depression. Even though the drug enjoyed immediate success, fear of side effects and the expectation of a new antidepressant soon to be released caused the manufacturer to take it off the market.

Meanwhile, a leading researcher in Switzerland, Ronald Kuhn, began to look for a drug to fight depression that would be nonstimulating in its action so that the person would feel better but not be specifically energized or agitated. Kuhn began by studying antihistamines, since the antihistamine chlorpromazine hydrochloride was already

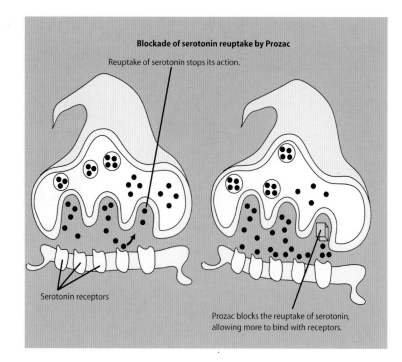

Blockade of serotonin reuptake by Prozac

Reuptake of serotonin stops its action.

Serotonin receptors

Prozac blocks the reuptake of serotonin, allowing more to bind with receptors.

being used to treat schizophrenia. Since it was a sedative, chlorpromazine had a calming effect, but it showed only a fair amount of success when treating depression; just calming the patient did not alleviate the major symptoms of depression.

By the end of 1957, Kuhn introduced a substance that would relieve depression. This drug was called imipramine hydrochloride and was the first of the antidepressants specifically designed to treat depression without overstimulating the recipient. When patients were taken off their old antidepressants and put on the new drug, appetites returned, and patients became more like themselves. Most important, they experienced no bizarre elevation of mood; in fact, when taken by nondepressed persons, they simply became sedated. This meant the drug would have little chance of becoming addictive.

Physicians were pleased with the results of the antidepressant. However, imipramine affected serotonin and norepinephrine, a neurotransmitter that did not need to be regulated. Treating neurotransmitters that do not need to be treated causes unnecessary side effects, such as sweating, heart palpitations, and dry mouth. Norepinephrine is the chemical that helps the body get ready for the "fight-or-flight" response to crisis. By increasing the amount of norepinephrine in the brain, imipramine kept the body in a perpetual state of readiness for action.

When researchers create drugs that work as they want them to but that have side effects that would be better eliminated, they normally continue their search for a better drug by creating chemicals similar to the earlier drugs. This type of research is called *homology* (from a Latin root meaning "same") because the researchers use the fundamental structure of the original chemical but try to change some part of the formula. Because this is the easiest route, much research starts here.

New drugs may also be developed using analogy. In this case, researchers look for other chemicals that will function similarly to the one previously used. For example, imipramine helped alleviate depression by affecting serotonin levels in the brain. However, the side effects somewhat outweighed the benefits of the drug. As a result, scientists looked for a drug that behaved like imipramine, in that it regulated serotonin levels, but that did not have the same side effects.

Some of the antidepressants closely related to imipramine were the monoamine oxidase inhibitors (MAOIs). As with the first antidepressants, MAOIs worked well in treating depression. Although researchers have proven that they inhibit monoamine oxidase, which works in the neurons of the brain, exactly how these drugs work is not understood

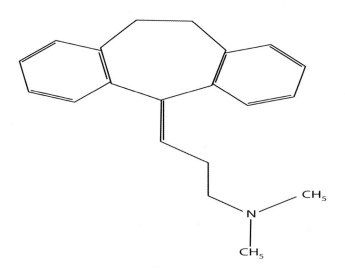

The three-ring chemical structure of a tricyclic drug.

Brand Name vs. Generic Name

Talking about psychiatric drugs can be confusing, because every drug has at least two names: its "generic name" and the "brand name" that the pharmaceutical company uses to market the drug. Generic names come from the drugs' chemical structures, while drug companies use brand names to inspire consumers' recognition and loyalty.

Here are the brand names and generic names for some common psychiatric drugs used to treat adjustment disorders:

Desyrel®	trazodone
Librium®	chlorodiazepoxide
Marplan®	isocarboxazid
Nardil®	phenelzine
Norpramin®	desipramine
Parnate®	tranylcypromine
Paxil®	paroxetine
Prozac®	fluoxetine
Tofranil®	imipramine
Valium®	diazepam
Xanax®	alprazolam
Zofran®	ondansetron
Zoloft®	sertraline

GLOSSARY

hypertension:
High blood
pressure.

fully. People with ***hypertension*** need to use MAOIs with caution, which limits its use for many patients.

Other antidepressants similar to imipramine are called tricyclics because of their triple-natured chemical structure—in this case, three carbon rings; these were said to have fewer side effects. Once it was discovered that the

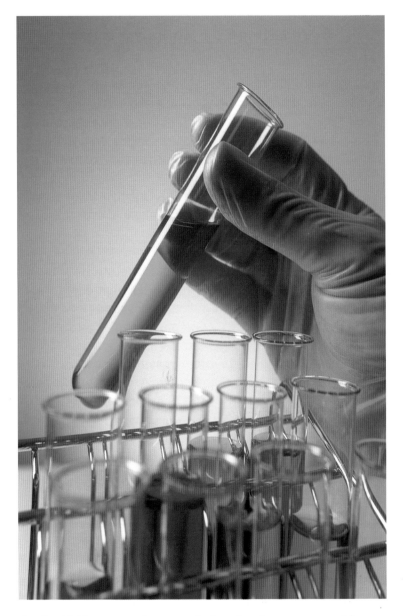

In the 1960s, researchers worked to develop a new antidepressant.

three-ring structure was a key to treating depression safely, scientists looked for other molecules that had the three chemical rings.

Many still believed that serotonin held the key to the majority of the mood problems of depression and other diseases. In the 1960s, Bryan Molloy, a Scottish chemist, and Ray Fuller, a *pharmacologist*, working together at Eli Lilly and Company, a pharmaceutical research and manufacturing firm, used a combination of studies to find the first SSRIs. Molloy was working on a heart regulator, while Fuller was testing new antidepressants on rats. Fuller convinced Molloy to work on chemicals that affected neurotransmitters in the brain. Molloy began by studying previous work on neurotransmitters and decided to start by experimenting with antihistamines. He based this work on a model presented by another researcher at Lily, Robert Rathbun. David Wong, a researcher in antibiotics, began studying the role of serotonin in mood regulation.

When Wong learned of the research performed by Solomon Snyder of Johns Hopkins University, he began using his technology on Molloy's antidepressants. Wong quickly found that they were like drugs already available. He continued his research by testing the chemicals that had failed in Molloy's tests. Of these, a compound labeled 82816 was found to block the uptake of serotonin without affecting other transmitters. The test was then run on Fuller's rats; it continued to work only on serotonin. The active ingredient in Prozac eventually came from these studies.

Prozac was introduced in 1988, about thirty years after the earliest antidepressants became available. Because of its specific effect on serotonin, Prozac offered relatively few side effects. Previous problems with the heart were not likely with Prozac, and most important, patients on Prozac did not feel lethargic or sedated.

Four Different Depressants

- alcoholic beverages
- narcotics
- barbiturates
- tranquilizers

Zoloft and the other SSRIs were developed after Prozac was. Although these drugs still have side effects, they are less severe than those experienced with other antidepressants. SSRIs regulate serotonin levels and affect the brain positively for those suffering from depression, panic, and even some severe forms of anxiety.

HELP FROM ANTIANXIETY MEDICATIONS

Sleeplessness often goes hand in hand with anxiety. Throughout history, many cultures have used some form of medication to induce sleep, mostly for those who were sleep-deprived due to illness or stress. Drugs such as seda-

Facts About Valium

Although it has helped millions of people, Valium has been one of the most widely abused prescribed drugs in history. Manufactured by Roche Pharmaceuticals in the early 1960s, the drug was largely unregulated and was often prescribed for problems that did not require the effects that Valium produced on the nervous system.

Because of its positive effects, researchers have worked to create antianxiety medications with a similar chemical structure but with fewer side effects than Valium. These include Xanax and Dalmane. In the United States today, Valium is only available with a doctor's prescription. In Mexico and Canada, however, the drug is available in mild doses over the counter.

One of the most serious side effects of antianxiety medications is their highly addictive nature. The need to take more in order to feel comfortable can lead to serious problems. These types of drugs need to be administered by a physician who can closely monitor the patient in order to prevent this from happening.

tives, hypnotics, and minor tranquilizers, slow down the central nervous system (CNS) by slowing down the mental and physical functions of the body. These drugs are commonly known as depressants. Because the nervous system is slowed, heart rate, lung function, and thought processes are also slowed down, leading to a delayed *reaction time*. For this reason, those taking depressants must be careful when performing activities that might harm themselves or others.

Used during ancient times, alcohol was the earliest depressant. It was first made from fermented honey, rice, or other foods as early as 5000 to 6000 B.C. By 2500 B.C., the book of Proverbs in the Bible listed the effects someone who drank too much would suffer:

GLOSSARY

reaction time: The amount of time necessary to react to a stimulus.

> Who has woe? Who has sorrow? Who has strife? Who has complaints? Who has needless bruises? Who has bloodshot eyes? Those who linger over wine, who go to sample bowls of mixed wine. Do not gaze at wine when it is red, when it sparkles in the cup, when it goes down smoothly! In the end it bites like a snake and poisons like a viper. Your eyes will see strange sights and your mind imagine confusing things. You will be like one sleeping on the high seas, lying on top of the rigging. "They hit me," you will say, "but I'm not hurt! They beat me, but I don't feel it! When will I wake up so I can find another drink?" (Proverbs 23: 29–35)

Like alcohol, *narcotics* were used by people to induce sleep, as well as to dull physical pain and relieve mental anguish. Opium is one of the oldest known narcotics, used originally by Sumerians living in what is now Iraq. Opium was so addictive that it caused wars; people would do nearly anything to maintain their habit.

In 1803, F. W. Serturner, a German pharmacist, developed morphine. At first this powerful narcotic was believed to be a wonderful, nonaddictive pain reliever. However, the invention of the hypodermic needle in 1855 made the use of morphine easy, and unfortunately, morphine was just as addictive as opium. So many people became addicted as a result that morphine use was a widespread problem.

The quest continued, however, to regulate the negative effects of depressants so that patients who suffered from mental and physical problems could gain the benefit of their positive effects. Barbiturates were the first antianxiety drugs prevalent during the early 1900s and are thought to have gotten the name "barbiturates" because on December 4, 1862, which is Saint Barbara's Day, Adolph von Bayer first *synthesized* the drug. Patients treated with these drugs noted feelings of intoxication much like those experienced with alcohol, including slurred speech, impaired judgment, and unsteadiness or lack of coordination. As with morphine, barbiturates soon caused addiction. Another problem—sometimes deadly—was that of overdose. Dependence tended to lead people to use more and more of the drug until eventually they forced their bodies into a coma—or death. Although some people could use barbiturates without becoming addicted, the number who had problems was high enough that researchers continued to look for alternative medication.

The 1960s saw the first benzodiazepines sold to the public. These were believed to be less addictive and less *sedating*. When used in higher doses, however, people taking these drugs had noticeable problems of oversedation: dizziness and confusion. Again, the drug led to dependence even when used at the prescribed doses. One positive aspect was that an overdose or overuse of this drug was usually not life threatening unless the patient combined benzodiazepines with other drugs or alcohol.

An increase in the ability to sleep, release from stressful feelings, and lessening of anxiety make the drugs an important part of certain therapies. In some cases, those suffering from adjustment disorders need the help these drugs offer to relieve stress and bring a sense of relaxation. Although the potential for addiction is present, working with a physician can make the use of an antianxiety drug a benefit to a patient who is suffering from a short-term disorder.

People who have low serotonin levels often experience:

- depression
- aggression
- increased risk of heart disease
- anxiety
- poor concentration
- impulsive behavior
- feelings of guilt
- food cravings
- alcoholism
- anger or rage

Adolescence is an exciting time, full of new opportunities and experiences. Communication between parents and teens often becomes strained, however; it may be difficult for an adolescent to explain to her parents what is bothering her.

3 | How Do the Drugs Work?

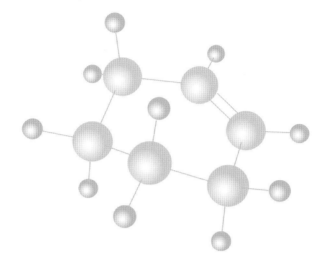

When Amy was fifteen, her mother and father gave her the good news that she would soon have a new brother or sister. Her parents were so excited about the new baby that Amy could not bring herself to tell them how she felt about the news. They had been so happy, just the three of them, for so long that Amy couldn't understand why her parents wanted another child. And she was embarrassed when a mother who was visibly pregnant came to her choral concerts and other school events.

Eventually, Amy stopped telling her parents about school activities. She spent more and more time at her friends' houses and avoided any talk or preparation for the baby's arrival. Amy dreaded all the changes that would come with a new baby, such as her parents having less time for her and spending more time with the baby. Rather than feeling excited about the new arrival, all Amy could think about was how it would change her life in negative ways.

Amy was angry, and she was taking it out on her parents. It wasn't until she was caught drinking at a party that her parents sought help for her. With the support of a psychologist and an antidepressant to help her gain control of her overwhelming emotions, Amy was able to talk through some of the things that had been bothering her.

Antidepressants work by changing the way the body reacts to certain situations. Difficult situations will still occur in a person's life; the antidepressant does not stop those things from happening. However, the antidepressant enables the person to feel more like him- or herself and thereby cope better with the difficult situations.

Tricyclic antidepressants block the passage of the serotonin and norepinephrine chemicals from the nerve end-

Some people who are suffering from an adjustment disorder may experience cravings for chocolate or other "junk" foods.

The human brain is an amazing and complex organ, seemingly limitless in capacity, even though it comprises only about two percent of the body's weight. As a part of the central nervous system, the brain coordinates the sensory information experienced by the body, allowing it to react to or process this stimulation. It also directs automatic functions in the body, such as heartbeat and respiration. It releases hormones and controls body temperature, hunger, and pleasure. Neurotransmitters have a great influence on mood and emotions, and can become imbalanced, causing different conditions such as depression, anxiety, or panic.

ings. When this happens, it causes a sedating, or calming, effect on the body. These drugs also elevate mood and help with pain. Tricyclic antidepressants increase mental alertness and physical activity and can even allow the user to sleep better. When the tricyclic antidepressant amitriptyline is combined with the tranquilizer perphenazine, the combination works to treat anxiety and depression specifically associated with adjustment disorder with mixed anxiety and depressed mood.

Individuals suffering from an adjustment disorder may experience food cravings at times. When they are depressed or upset, they may find themselves overeating on chocolate cookies, brownies, potato chips, or other "junk" foods. Lower levels of serotonin may cause this erratic eating, because the brain will do what it needs to raise the serotonin level. When not enough serotonin neurotransmitters get to the receptors, messages do not get passed from cell to cell properly. As a result, the brain opens more receptors to grab as many serotonin neurotransmitters as possible. If that doesn't work, it may produce the cravings that lead to eating things like whole bags of chocolate chip cookies in order to try to raise serotonin levels through food intake. Carbohydrates, which are present in many sugary or starchy foods

like cakes and potato chips, cause serotonin levels to rise. People who eat too many sugary desserts or drink sugar-laden soft drinks when they are upset may be suffering from low serotonin levels.

Because of something known as the ***blood–brain bar-rier***, serotonin cannot be given directly, so it can't affect the brain neurons as needed. Instead, serotonin administered directly into the system affects all of the neurotransmitters, which causes increased side effects.

Antianxiety medications are different from antidepressant medications in that they affect the CNS by enhancing the functions of GABA, the major inhibitor of nerve transmissions between the brain and the CNS. It acts to slow down the passage of messages between nerve cells. Whereas in depression, messages are not being passed fast enough, with anxiety attacks, the messages are being passed too quickly. Antianxiety medications, such as benzodiazepines, are fast acting, so the patient experiences relief almost immediately. Because of this, these drugs work well in emergencies or for short-term therapy.

Tranquilizers are taken orally, and once in the bloodstream, they are moved to the liver where they are ***metabolized***. From the liver, the useable parts of the drug attach to proteins in the blood and are transported to the brain. There they affect the normal functioning of the brain by

Zoloft and Prozac are two types of SSRIs. Just as the thermostat in your home keeps the temperature constant, these drugs, and others like them, work to keep serotonin at a productive level within the brain. And they accomplish this without making the patient too lethargic and sleepy to accomplish everyday tasks.

Electroshock therapy was once commonly used as a treatment for depression, and in a few cases, it is still used today. Some researchers now believe that both serotonin and electroshock treatments cause new cells to be created in the brain. If this hypothesis is correct, the drug researchers might shift the attention from drugs that affect neurotransmission to drugs that stimulate the creation of neurons in the brain.

calming or repressing it, thus slowing down brain functions. By sending messages to the brain's hypothalamus, where anxiety, fear, and anger are felt, tranquilizers regulate the messages sent to the rest of the body.

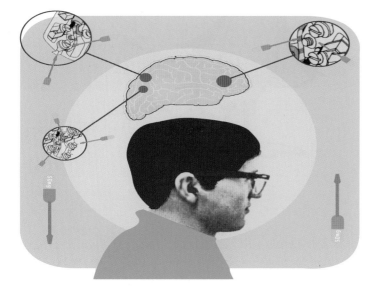

Our brains receive messages from many sources—from our senses, from other parts of our bodies, and from medications in our bloodstreams.

People sometimes are reluctant to take psychiatric drugs for fears others will think they are "odd ducks"! In reality, taking drugs that affect the mind is no different from taking medicine for other parts of the body.

When taking a tranquilizer, feelings of fear are lessened, and the patient does not experience the impending sense of doom often felt during an anxiety attack. This lessening of symptoms allows a counselor to work on the issues a patient is dealing with when suffering from adjustment disorder so that she or he is better able to cope with them. Tranquilizers are often prescribed in addition to an antianxiety medication or an antidepressant for a patient who suffers adjustment disorder while becoming accustomed to a major change in his or her life. However, people taking these drugs must be monitored closely because of the potential to become addicted.

Sometimes people are afraid to take medication that affects the brain because they feel it makes them seem like they aren't strong enough to take care of themselves or that they are crazy. However, psychiatric medication may help a person cope better with the stresses in her life. No one would argue that a person with an infection didn't need an antibiotic to get better. In a similar way, antianxiety and antidepressant medications help a person feel better so that he can live a normal life. The brain can be helped back into a more efficient state with the help of antidepressants or antianxiety medications. This can mean the difference between healthy living and living under the influence of an imbalance within the brain.

If someone no longer enjoys the activities she once did, that may be a symptom of an adjustment disorder.

4 | Treatment Description

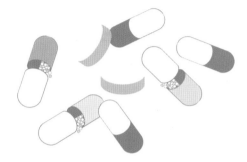

The mother of a twenty-year-old noticed that when her daughter returned from a semester abroad she no longer seemed to enjoy the fun parts of her life. Megan went to school and continued to perform as well as she had before, but she didn't seem to enjoy any of the extracurricular activities she had found pleasure in before she went away. The mother continued to watch her daughter whenever she was home and listened as they spoke on the phone. She kept hearing things like, "That's just life" and "I guess it just doesn't get any better than this."

By the end of the semester, the mother was worried about Megan and asked their physician his opinion. He had known Megan for years, and he thought that perhaps they should make an appointment during her Thanksgiving break. When he began questioning Megan, he learned that she had had a few anxiety attacks since she had been home. While she was away, Megan had felt a freedom she had not experienced before. The culture where she lived was not so

Life's demands may sometimes seem overwhelming. Even if we had twelve hands, we'd never be able to accomplish every-thing—and the stress interferes with our ability to cope.

mindful of the time, and relationships were more important than grades or appointments. Once she was back home, she felt that she couldn't find a balance between the two lives and wondered if she would always long for a less stressful life. At the same time, she had goals for herself that she didn't think she wanted to give up.

Her physician helped her see that this was, in many ways, a part of growing into the responsibilities of adulthood. He felt she did not need to suffer from the anxiety, especially with finals approaching. He prescribed an anti-anxiety medication and was able to set up a series of appointments with a psychologist who helped Megan through this transition in her life.

When someone is suffering from a psychiatric or emotional problem, a first step is to find a physician or mental health professional who can reach an accurate diagnosis of the disorder.

Many people who are under a lot of stress have trouble remembering details like numbers, dates, and names. Some physicians prescribe a low dose of an antidepressant, such as Prozac, to help the brain function more efficiently. As we have already learned, when the neurons can receive neurotransmitters properly, there is an elevation in the brain's efficiency. Physicians have found that symptoms involving thinking or dizziness, if untreated, tend to lead to anxiety, panic, and mood swings. They are more likely to treat them with a lower dosage drug and try to control the immediate symptoms before they lead to a larger problem.

MENTAL HEALTH PROFESSIONALS

Mental health professionals are people who have chosen a career in which they help people with mental health disorders. Each of the various types of mental health professionals has a different type of training.

Psychologists

Clinical psychologists must have a Ph.D. degree—but they do not have a medical degree. As with all mental health professionals, they receive hundreds of hours in supervised practice. They also spend a year in an *internship* before becoming eligible to take licensing examinations. They specialize in the treatment of mental disorders, and they may also have special training in conducting and interpreting research on the treatment of mental disorders. Because they do not have a medical degree, they cannot prescribe medications.

Psychiatrists

A psychiatrist is a medical doctor who has completed medical school, including a *residency* setting where she worked with mental illness instead of physical illness. In most cases, psychiatrists are the only mental health professionals who can prescribe medications. Because of this privilege, psychiatrists often work with other types of mental health professionals. Counselors and other therapists often refer patients to them to determine whether the patients need medication to help with their condition or whether they have a medical condition that requires treatment.

Psychiatric Nurses

Psychiatric nurses are licensed registered nurses; they have a minimum of a master's degree, and they are certified nationally. The credential for advanced clinical practice is a

Psychiatric nurses are one kind of mental health professional who can diagnose psychiatric disorders. Advanced practice psychiatric nurses can also prescribe medication.

certified specialist (CS), or they may have an APRN—advanced practice, registered nurse. Some psychiatric nurses with special training can prescribe medications for the treatment of mental disorders, as well as administer therapy. Like the other mental health professionals, they are required to have extensive supervised clinical experience before they can be licensed.

Marriage and Family Therapists

MFTs (also called MFCCs—marriage, family, and child counselors) have graduate training (either a master's degree or doctorate) in marriage and family therapy. They too have received hundreds of hours of supervised clinical experience over a period of at least two years. Most states license, certify, or regulate MFTs. Although these therapists specialize in treating psychological problems within the family context, they also counsel individual children and adults.

Licensed Clinical Social Workers

Clinical social workers have either a master's degree or doctorate in social work. They have concentrated in clinical course work and undergone a supervised graduate clinical field internship, as well as at least two years of postgraduate supervised clinical social work employment. They work to prevent and to treat mental disorders.

Counselors

Counselors usually have at least a master's degree, which included field training and an internship. In the United States, forty-four states require that a counselor be licensed in his field.

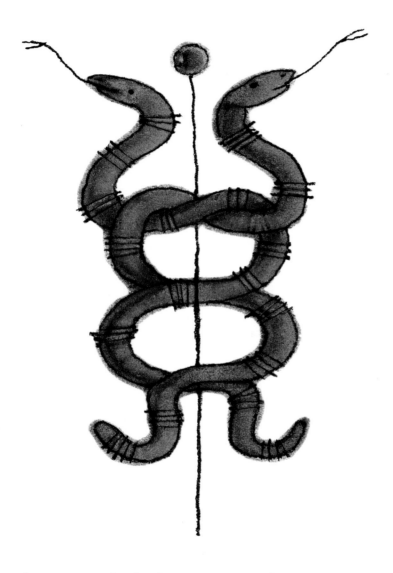

There are many kinds of mental health professionals, but only licensed medical practitioners—physicians, psychiatrists, and advanced practice nurses—can prescribe medication.

During the initial session the mental health professional will assess the client—but the client will also have the opportunity to assess the mental health professional. The client should expect from the first meeting opportunities to:

- Assess the clinician's training and credentials. He should be licensed—and if he isn't, he should have a licensed supervisor who will meet with him to discuss the case on a regular basis.
- Inquire about the therapist's theoretical point of view (for example, does this therapist practice only one type of therapy—psychodynamic, cognitive-behavioral—or is she experienced in various types?) Some disorders do well with any type of therapy, but others require very specific therapies. The client should make sure that the therapist either uses various forms of therapy or uses the one most appropriate for his situation.
- Assess the therapist's level of experience—how many similar cases has he treated? How many years has she been practicing? The confidence with which the mental health professional answers these questions will help the client decide whether she wants to invest in this relationship, a relationship that might be one of the most important relationships in her life.
- Obtain some relief. Although the initial session is very structured and aimed at helping the therapist gain information, the client should feel better afterward—first, because the first session is over and a great deal of stress and worry has probably been associated with thinking about this first meeting; second, the client has taken the first step toward improved mental health and just knowing this will make him feel better; and third, even though the mental health professional has spent the session obtaining information, she will also provide the client with some education about what to expect in the days ahead (and knowledge often helps to dispel anxiety).

INITIAL EVALUATION

Once a person has chosen a mental health professional, she can expect to undergo an initial evaluation at her first appointment. This is also known as the intake evaluation or the assessment. This first face-to-face meeting between the person and the therapist is usually scheduled to last at least an hour and a half. (Later, "therapy hours" will traditionally last fifty minutes.)

During this evaluation, the mental health professional obtains as much information as possible about the patient, including:

- Demographic information (age, education, family structure, etc.). Sometimes therapists will ask clients to complete a mail-in form with demographic questions, which saves time during the initial assessment. Other mental health professionals may prefer to fill in the form during the initial appointment so that they can discuss parts of the form as it is filled in.
- Family history, including any history of psychiatric illness in the family. There are at least two important reasons for this: first, many mental disorders have a hereditary component, and second, growing up with people with certain mental illnesses can predispose individuals to develop psychiatric problems.
- History of current problem. The therapist will ask questions such as when the symptoms began, what the symptoms are, and how they are interfering with the person's daily functioning.
- Psychiatric history. The mental health professional will determine whether the person has ever experienced these or other psychiatric symptoms before; if so, the therapist will ask more questions regarding these past events.

- Mental status exam. This can take various forms. The therapist is trying to assess level of intelligence, cognitive functioning, and so on.

Based on this information, the therapist will develop a plan that includes:

- Obtaining other information. This may mean medical records, past psychiatric records, or accounts from other family members. For each of these, the therapist is required to request your permission in writing (or if you are a minor, your parent's or legal guardian's permission).
- Type of treatment that you need (counseling, behavior therapy, etc.).
- If you need medication immediately. If so, you may be referred to a psychiatrist for the medication (but

When a young, aggressive male has an adjustment disorder, his symptoms will likely appear different from those of a quiet, older woman.

Some mental health professionals do not believe that adjustment disorders need to be treated. With time, most people will recover on their own from an adjustment disorder, and therapy costs money and time. However, therapy can provide support during a difficult time and may speed up the recovery process. In cases in which the adjustment disorder is causing family conflict, the advantages of seeking therapy are likely to outweigh the disadvantages, since family difficulties may in turn grow worse, creating a vicious cycle that prolongs the problem.

the other mental health professional will continue to work with you also). If you don't need drug treatment at once, a counselor or other mental health professional may work with you for a few sessions before making a referral to a psychiatrist.

- If the mental health professional you chose is the best qualified person to continue to work with you. Sometimes, because of the specific circumstances of the client or therapist, mental health professionals will refer clients to other therapists or mental health centers that specialize in the type of problem for which the client needs help.

When a patient is diagnosed with adjustment disorder, the first step in regaining health is to treat the symptoms. This is accomplished by classifying the illness under its subtypes and specifiers. Each person will have different symptoms, and these help physicians and psychiatrists to diagnose psychiatric disorders more effectively.

For instance, when a young man with a disturbance of emotions and conduct is evaluated, he may need a different prescription than an older woman who is suffering an ad-

justment disorder with anxiety. In the case of the young person, he is defiant and attracting attention to himself and his actions by skipping school, "egging" teachers' cars, and reckless driving. By contrast, the woman draws little attention to herself as she slowly withdraws from social functions until she only leaves her home when it is absolutely necessary.

In both cases, however, the use of a psychiatric drug may allow the patient to more easily enter into an open relationship with a counselor. After evaluating the patient physically and mentally, the physician may prescribe either an antianxiety medication or an antidepressant. Either of these treatments will be used short term as a vehicle to help the patient better understand and work toward a quick recovery. In counseling sessions, both individuals will be helped

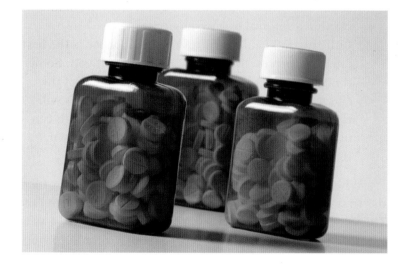

Always tell your doctor about any medications you are taking, even if it is only aspirin or some other over-the-counter remedy.

Precautions for Taking Zoloft and Prozac

These are problems you need to speak to your physician about before you choose this treatment.

1. Always inform your doctor of any other medications, prescription or over-the-counter, that you are taking.
2. Consuming alcoholic beverages while on these medications is not recommended.
3. Caution should be taken when using:
   Diazipam®, an antianxiety and sedative treatment.
   Digitoxin®, a heart treatment.
   Lithium, a manic-depressive and bipolar treatment.
   Other psychiatric antidepressants, such as Elavil® and thioridazine tablets.
   Over-the-counter cold remedies.
   Warfarin®, an anticoagulant.
4. Serious, and sometimes fatal, reactions can occur when taking an MAOI such as Nardil®, Parnate®, and Marplan®. Allow fourteen days between discontinuing MAOI therapy and beginning Zoloft or Prozac.
5. A rash can be the sign of a serious medical condition for those taking medication. See your physician immediately if you develop a rash while taking the medication.
6. Inform your physician of any reactions to other antidepressants.

to identify the original stressor and be taught coping skills so that he or she will return to normal and possibly avoid a recurrence of adjustment problems in the future.

SSRIs can be used in treating adjustment disorders. This group of antidepressants, although a relatively new member of the antidepressant family, can be used in combination with the tricyclic antidepressants to give greater re-

"Off-Label" Prescriptions

The FDA bases its approval on specific research results. Sometimes, a particular use for a drug may have been thoroughly researched by many studies, while other uses lack the same amount of research. In that case, the drug label will only include the uses that have met the FDA's stringent research requirements. Physicians, however, may continue to prescribe that drug for other "off-label" uses.

---

lief than either medication alone. Because SSRIs cause an increase in the action of serotonin in the brain, they reduce fatigue and increase energy, thus sometimes making it harder to sleep at night. This can aggravate anyone who is already feeling physical or mental symptoms.

Prozac, a common SSRI used to treat depression, can be started with a 20-milligram dose but should not exceed 80 milligrams per day. While this drug has not been approved for children by the FDA, those eighteen years of age and younger are often prescribed a dose between 5 milligrams and 40 milligrams. For those who have trouble with feelings of anxiety, one pill can be taken every other day. This course of treatment is possible because the medication remains in the body for several days after discontinuing the drug and has even been found in the blood weeks after terminating use. Thus, a more sensitive person can get the same benefits on an every-other-day dose.

When treating depression, some patients may experience an improvement of symptoms within two weeks, but for most it takes up to four weeks. Those who have trouble

When a particular drug is commonly prescribed for disorders not approved by the FDA, that is called "off-label" use. Many drugs are commonly prescribed for off-label purposes.

sleeping while taking Prozac should take their dose in the morning. This is sometimes the only adjustment needed to alleviate this problem.

One of the most important precautions to remember about taking the SSRIs Zoloft or Prozac is that there can be a dangerous—even fatal—reaction between one or the other of these drugs and MAOIs. If you are presently taking or have taken within the last two weeks any of the MAOIs, drugs such as Nardil, Parnate, and Marplan, do not begin taking Zoloft or Prozac without consulting your physician.

Major depression is present if five or more of the following symptoms are a problem during the same two-week period. One of the symptoms must be either a depressed mood or loss of interest. Other symptoms include:

- Feeling sad or depressed most of the day.
- Significant appetite or weight change combined with either an increase or decrease in eating.
- Sleeping too much or too little.
- Feeling flustered, irritated, or inactive and not wanting to do anything physical.
- Loss of interest in things that you used to enjoy.
- Feeling extremely tired, like you have no energy.
- Feeling worthless or excessively or inappropriately guilty.
- Difficulty concentrating or thinking clearly.
- Thoughts of suicide, attempts of suicide, or morbid thoughts of death.

Adapted from The University of Pennsylvania Health System at www.pennhealth.com.

Young people or adults who experience anxiety, depression, or other adjustment symptoms and are not treated may begin to treat themselves with alcohol or illegal drugs. These are far more dangerous and likely to cause more serious problems with addiction.

Zoloft is approved for depression and panic disorder. The usual initial dosage for adults taking Zoloft is 50 milligrams once a day, either in the morning or the evening. For those having a problem with insomnia, Zoloft should be taken in the morning. It is available in 25-milligram, 50-milligram, and 100-milligram scored tablets that can be broken in half to allow adjustment of dosages. Those who are sensitive to medications should start out at 25 milligrams, which can then be increased after a week or more of treatment but should not exceed 200 milligrams per day. A dose may be crushed and mixed with food or left in tablet form. Taking Zoloft without food causes no problems, but taking it with food does enhance absorption.

As with Prozac, Zoloft usually takes about four to six weeks to begin minimizing depression, but it could take up to eight weeks for some people. If a dose of Zoloft is missed, it must be taken as soon as possible. If several hours have passed, the dose should be skipped, as no one should ever take a double dose. The pills are best stored at room temperature. The physician should always be informed of any changes that occur, good or bad, while taking Zoloft.

There have been many trials done studying the effectiveness and safety of Prozac and Zoloft. They are considered safe to use, but must be monitored regularly by a doctor because each person reacts to medication differently. Some people are so sensitive that they need to adjust their

dosages and start at very low levels, moving slowly up to the lowest effective dose. Other SSRIs are also frequently used for adjustment disorders. Practitioners have found them to be helpful for these cases, but the drugs have not been studied extensively for this condition; therefore, they do not have FDA approval.

Tricyclic antidepressants are prescribed in lower doses for adjustment disorder than they are when used for treating depression. Those suffering sleep problems because of stress benefit greatly when they can correct even that one problem. Instead of experiencing **nonrestorative** sleep, the antidepressant allows the patient to experience the deep sleep known as delta-wave sleep. The medication also allows the nerve cells of the brain to access higher levels of serotonin, which causes the person to feel more relaxed.

GLOSSARY

nonrestorative:
Not bringing back
to or putting back
into a former or
original state.

One of the most commonly used tricyclic antidepressants in the treatment of adjustment disorder is Elavil. Although the FDA-approved dosage is 50 to 150 milligrams at bedtime, some practitioners have found that as little as 10 milligrams about two to three hours before bedtime helps many patients experience relaxed muscles and a restful sleep. Lower doses are usually used for adolescents and elderly patients. Elavil stays in the system for about eight hours, so it also helps to take the medicine earlier so that there are no drowsy feelings in the morning. It can take three to six weeks for Elavil to reach its full potential; however, it can be taken on an as-needed basis and still work for some patients.

Other tricyclic antidepressants that are used to treat adjustment disorder include imipramine tablets, nortriptyline capsules, Norpramin, and Desyrel. Depression may be helped with most of these, except Desyrel, which seems to alleviate sleeplessness and pain more than any other symptoms.

*Tricyclic antidepressants are often prescribed to treat adjust-
ment disorders.*

Two new combinations of tricyclic antidepressants and SSRIs are Effexor and Serzone. However, these may be difficult to regulate because of their varied effects on sleep. Since it may take more than a month before a person even begins to respond to these drugs, they are usually taken for three to six months before reevaluation by a physician.

Antianxiety drugs can also prove helpful in the treatment of adjustment disorder because of their ability to produce immediate results. Most people feel better within hours of taking their first dose. The different types of tranquilizers include Valium, Librium, Tranxene, and Xanax. They are used as muscle relaxants and sleep aids. It is important to keep in mind that antianxiety medication tends to be addicting and can be difficult to discontinue. Be sure to follow the doctor's prescription, and do not mix the prescription with alcohol. One way to monitor the tolerance of the medication is by the level taken. The patient is becoming tolerant if the dosage has to be raised.

Valium is prescribed to children and adolescents in daily dosages from 4 to 10 milligrams divided into three or four doses. This may be tapered off as the young person begins to respond to therapy and feels that he is resolving the stressful issues in his life. Xanax and Ativan, both medications with short-term effects, are prescribed in 0.5- to 6-milligram doses. These can also be taken three times a day. (The recommended beginning dose for an adult is 0.5 milligrams three times a day; depending on the person's response, the dose can be increased every three to four days by no more than one milligram.) Although all of these drugs work within thirty minutes of taking them, they wear off fast, so it is necessary to dose more often during the day.

Treatment should always include regular evaluation by a physician. If, after a month of treatment, the patient is having positive results, the medication is usually continued for a few more months. At that point, the patient and physician may choose to use the tricyclic antidepressant every other night. Eventually, the patient will use the drug only as needed, such as when the patient has not been sleeping well for a few nights in a row or when she is experiencing other stresses at work or school. During the entire course of treatment, and perhaps afterward, the patient should also work with a counselor in order to identify and better cope with any stressors.

Antidepressants are not addictive. The adult or child patient does not need to worry about becoming dependent. Antianxiety medications (benzodiazepines) can, however, produce both *physiological* and psychological dependence. Benzodiazepines are typically used short term until an SSRI becomes effective, or they may be used long term for occasional "break-through" anxiety. (If the person finds she needs to take a benzodiazepine more frequently, she should notify her prescribing clinician, since the SSRI may need to be increased.) When benzodiazepines are abused or used improperly, addiction can become a problem. As with any drug, it is important to follow the advice of a medical pratitioner.

G L O S S A R Y

physiological: Characteristic of or appropriate to an organism's healthy or normal functioning.

The stresses young people encounter at school may sometimes be severe enough to cause an adjustment disorder.

5 | Case Studies

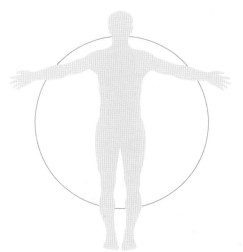

As we have learned, adjustment disorders are short-term mood disorders that are triggered by a particular stressor occurring in the sufferer's life. While the fact that the symptoms are short term does not make the sufferer feel much better, it does make the studying of the disorder more difficult. In many cases, the sufferer does not even report the problem to a physician unless the symptoms become unbearable.

A typical case may involve an adolescent having a difficult time at school with a teacher. The young person knows why he is feeling depressed and unhappy, but figures he just has to endure the situation because he can't do anything about the teacher who harasses him. In one case study, a young man said he spent a whole year of school in agony over a math teacher. The student dreaded having to go to school every day and sometimes actually felt sick to his stomach. He dreamed of ways to get out of that class and prayed that school would be delayed so classes would be shorter, or better yet canceled. He took every opportunity to miss school and even skipped a few days without getting caught. Naturally, his grades fell that year and he did not like school.

However, the following year, his classes were back to normal. In fact, he had a few teachers he liked so well that he looked forward to school. He had no more stomachaches, and he stopped skipping school.

Reports like these can be helpful to others who are experiencing an adjustment disorder. As individuals understand they are not alone, they are not "weird," and that help is available, they may also seek help and avoid further complications. In some cases, those who experience an adjustment disorder that takes the form of anxiety, depression, or some other mood disturbance may eventually face a chronic disorder because they did not pursue help earlier. Case studies

If you are having difficulty coping with the stress of school, family, or other aspects of your life, you are not weird! Other people experience the same difficulties.

Some Information About Those Who Suffer from Adjustment Disorder

- Both males and females suffer from the disorder.
- Adjustment disorders affect people at almost any age, although there is a high incidence during transitions in life such as adolescence, midlife, menopause, and retirement.
- More than five percent of all persons treated in hospitals or as outpatients are diagnosed with one of the subtypes of adjustment disorder.

---

offer help and encouragement to individuals troubled with adjustment difficulties.

Morgan had worked hard for three years on the school newspaper. He was a senior this year and expected that he would be the editor in chief. However, when the school year began, the students were surprised to find that the journalism teacher had become ill over the summer and a younger teacher had taken over the position. In the past, the instructor had allowed the students working on the paper to vote for the editor in chief. Miss Verne, being new to the school and enthusiastic about doing a good job, had instead spent hours reading past issues of the newspaper and surveying records on the editors and other students involved in its production. She asked each person interested in the position to write a paper titled "How I Would Run the School Newspaper."

After examining the essays, Miss Verne chose a sophomore girl as editor in chief. Morgan couldn't believe he had put so much effort into the paper for the past three years

only to end up editor of the sports page during his senior year—but he refused to let anyone else know how he felt. At home, he acted like it didn't matter. When his best friend, Jamie, started criticizing the new journalism teacher, Morgan just told him to forget it.

Before long, though, Morgan had an argument with the new editor in chief over an article he had written. Another time, he felt the placement of a key picture on the sports page ruined the entire article, and again he argued with the editor in chief. By the end of the first semester, Morgan, the editor in chief, and Miss Verne were constantly at odds with each other. He ended up with a C in his journalism class.

Morgan gave up. He didn't care about the paper, especially the sports page. He was rude to everyone in journalism class. One day he became so angry he ripped up a layout page and not only left class but left the school. He was suspended for three days, and now his parents became involved. They admitted they were worried, as Morgan had never been so down before. He had always worked hard to keep his grades up because he wanted to enter a college journalism program and knew that competition was tough.

After hearing this, Miss Verne also overheard some kids talking about Morgan, and she finally understood the problem. She went to the principal and he, the guidance counselor, Miss Verne, and Morgan's parents reviewed the problem. Morgan was asked to meet with the school psychologist. They discussed his disappointment, his reaction, and things he might have chosen to do to help the situation. Morgan explained how angry he had been and how he felt everything he had worked for had been ruined. Morgan soon realized that he had overreacted and would have been better off speaking to his teacher. He learned some important skills that helped him to deal with professional relationships as he pursued his journalism career throughout college.

Everyone copes differently with life's tensions.

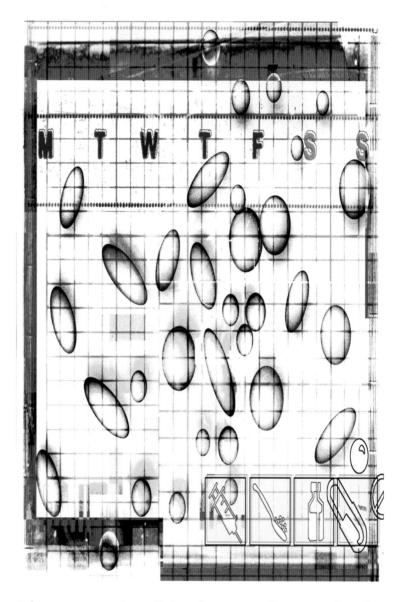

When someone is suffering from an adjustment disorder, medication may help her better cope with the demands of a busy life.

Losing one's temper more easily than usual may be one symptom of an adjustment disorder.

Morgan had experienced an adjustment disorder. It was not a permanent condition, and he did not need drug therapy to help him recover from his emotional difficulties. He did, however, need the support of family, teachers, and other professionals to help him move on.

Moving to a different community and changing schools can be another tremendous stressor for some young people. The effects of a move that takes them away from friends and extended family may be overlooked in the midst of the entire family's tension. A father who must begin a new job and a mother who looks for new employment or involvement in church and social organizations may be so busy they fail to notice how their children are coping. The search for new health care, automobile repair, baby-sitters, hair care, banks, grocery stores, and church is time consuming and stressful.

Margie was nineteen when her parents moved to the Midwest. She was a freshman in a college back East where they had lived. On her first visit home, she was happy to be with her family; she helped her mother pick out curtains and a bedspread for her new room, and she spent some time arranging her things. The time went quickly since she was only home for a weekend visit, and she felt fine about the move.

Her second visit was during spring break. This time, she spent eight days at her new home. When she first arrived, she was tired, and a few quiet days with her parents and younger sister were a great reprieve from her hectic pace at school. However, she soon realized she had no friends nearby, and she had very little opportunity to meet any. She wasn't in school here, she wasn't home long enough to get to know any young people at church, and she began to feel lonely.

When she returned to school, Margie began plans to look for a job in her old hometown and made arrangements to live with her best friend there. Once she had things arranged, she approached her parents—but they would not agree to the plan. Margie could not imagine a summer in the Midwest, and she could not believe how unreasonable her parents were not to allow her to stay with her friend's family. She stopped calling home. When her parents called her, she would barely talk to them. Although they had always been close, Margie felt they were being cruel and irrational. She just couldn't do what they wanted, so she continued her plans for a summer back home.

People who suffer from adjustment disorder need to understand that even "good" changes—such as marriage, a new baby, or a promotion to a better job—can cause a great deal of stress. Each of these events brings with it change and adjustment. These adjustments are sometimes more successful than others. Although time can help the person get used to the change, counseling and medication can often help speed the process along and avoid more severe problems later.

A new home, a new baby, a new job are all positive life changes—but they can still cause physical and emotional tension.

Clinical depression is an ongoing, serious psychiatric disorder. The depression caused by an adjustment disorder is short-term, brought on by a particular event or circumstance.

Antagonism mounted between Margie and her parents. She began missing classes, not sleeping at night, and spending her days trying to catch up on lost sleep. Her parents felt helpless because they were so far away. Even though Margie believed her parents were wrong, the more she pulled away, doing exactly what she knew they didn't want her to do, the worse she felt. It wasn't until she dragged herself to an English class on the wrong day that her professor asked if Margie needed help with anything. Margie, tired, anxious, and upset, told her professor the whole story. The English professor introduced Margie to one of the college's counselors, who was able to help her devise a plan suitable to her and her parents. She referred Margie to a psychiatrist, who

Depression occurs in varying degrees within individuals. There is a definite difference between reactive depression and clinical depression. Reactive depression, or adjustment disorder, occurs when an individual has an understandable or significant loss or a change in circumstances. In general, people can recognize the source of their anguish and can move past the negative feelings more readily with counseling and possibly the use of medication.

Clinical depression is usually associated with what might be called profound or deep loss that may be based on childhood trauma or patterns that need to be relearned and helped with medications and psychotherapy.

prescribed a mild antidepressant to help Margie regain a regular sleeping schedule. The counselor also helped Margie see that although she believed her problem stemmed from her parents' unreasonable actions, *her* reaction to the move was at the base of her problems. With new coping skills, Margie was able to resolve her emotional issues and continue her education without any further adjustment disorder.

More than one million children endure their parents' divorce each year. Divorce begins long before it becomes a legal battle, and many times tensions continue after the final separation as children realize their family unit has been dissolved.

A study performed at the University of Washington in Seattle investigated the interaction between parenting and the temperament of the child as a predictor of adjustment problems for children during a divorce. The twenty-three mothers and their children, who ranged in age from nine to twelve, had experienced divorce within the last

Many children in today's world have to adjust to their parents' separation or divorce.

two years. The mothers and the children were questioned in relation to parenting skills, temperament, and adjustment variables. Parental rejection led to adjustment problems for those children who were emotionally less positive, and inconsistent discipline caused more of an adjustment problem for those children high in *impulsivity*. These findings suggest that children who are high in impulsivity may be at greater risk for developing problems, whereas positive emotional health may protect children, decreasing the risk of adjustment problems in response to negative parenting.

What these studies hope to find are better ways to treat and care for adjustment problems before they become a behavioral or adjustment disorder. It is thought that by giving parents and others information on how and why certain personalities react to certain situations, some difficulties may be lessened or avoided altogether.

Another study was done to determine the characteristics of military personnel who had been diagnosed with adjustment disorder. The desire was to be better able to give appropriate treatment according to specific symptoms. The thirty-six military personnel who participated met the criteria in the *Diagnostic and Statistical Manual of Mental Disorders*, fourth edition (DSM-IV) for adjustment disorder. The control group consisted of twenty-four age-matched participants. The participants were interviewed individually and participated in the **Wechsler Adult Intelligence Scale-Revised** test. They also completed questionnaires, including information on area statistical data, parental bonding information, personality information, and a health survey.

The data showed a significant difference in personality and parental bonding attitudes between those suffering with adjustment disorder and the control group. Those

Adjustment disorders have a serious side that cannot be ignored: a percentage of those suffering from this disorder battle thoughts of suicide. Many of the recorded diagnoses of adjustment disorder come from those who are admitted to the hospital or who are treated in emergency rooms for attempted suicide.

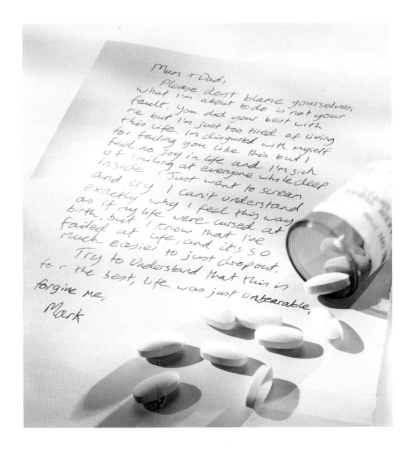

Suicide is a serious risk factor for adjustment disorders.

A positive relationship with parents is one element of good mental health.

soldiers with higher **neuroticism**, lower **extraversion**, and maternal overprotection had an increased risk of suffering from adjustment disorder.

In a report published in September 2002, it was estimated that between five and 21 percent of adult psychiatric consultations were for patients diagnosed with adjustment disorder. A little more than seven percent of the inpatient hospital admissions were for adjustment disorder as well. With this information, a study was then performed to compare the readmission rates for adjustment disorder with other mood disorders. In order to gain the needed information, data was used from the review of ten years of readmission data, including the diagnostic categories of adjustment dis-

Plants grow better in natural sunlight—and people do better when their work patterns follow the natural cycle of light and darkness.

orders, major depressive disorder (single episode and recurrent), dysthymia (a long-term chronic depression), and anxiety disorders.

The researchers found that admission diagnosis was a significant predictor of readmission. Those diagnosed with adjustment disorder had significantly fewer readmissions than those who were diagnosed with one of the other mood disorders. The study showed that those with a correct diagnosis of adjustment disorder did not need to be hospitalized once they understood from what they were suffering.

The *Shiftwork International Newsletter* reported in May 1996 that there was a significant link between shiftwork and depression. Shiftwork refers to a work schedule in which a long stretch of hours (or days) are worked before another long period of time off. For example, many police officers work shifts in which they are on duty for twelve hours for three days, have three days off, and then go back to work for three days again.

A survey revealed that depression was higher among shiftworkers than it was in the general public. The survey was divided into questions on three categories of depression that a shiftworker might suffer. One was depression directly related to shiftwork; the second was reactive depression, probably exacerbated by shiftwork; and the third was reactive depression linked to a major life event. Reactive depression is adjustment disorder with the subcategory of depressed mood.

In answer to the question, "All other things being equal, would you have preferred to give up working shifts and get a daytime job?" three out of seven whose depression was connected to a major life event responded, "Definitely yes."

Case studies like these help researchers and individuals better understand how adjustment disorders can be treated. They may also offer insight on how general health issues—such as eating properly, sleeping, and exercise—relate to adjustment disorders.

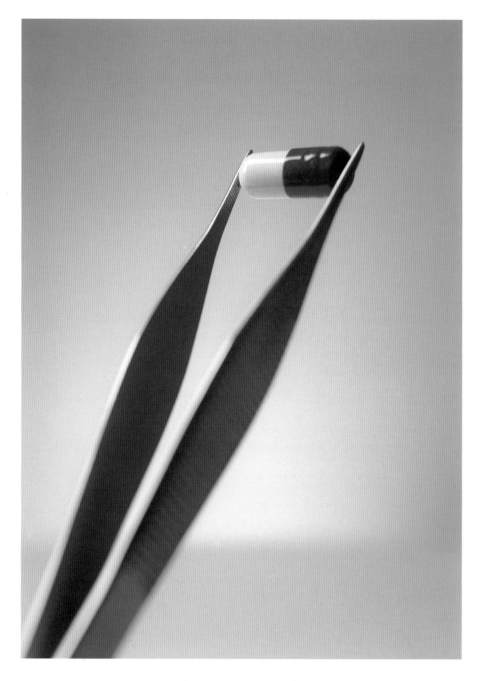

There is no magic pill!

6 | Risks and Side Effects of Drug Therapy

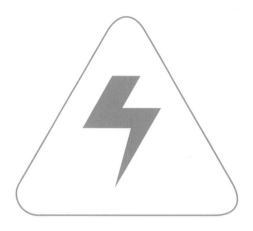

Drug therapy can offer help and hope to those who suffer from an adjustment disorder. However, no medication is a "magic pill." The human body is a complicated system, and psychiatric medications are powerful chemicals that can throw out of balance one part of the body's system—even while they help correct another area. Even after years of research and refinement, psychiatric drugs still have side effects and risks.

One of the specific problems in treating psychiatric disorders is that there are a number of neurotransmitter systems within the brain and many times they have a role in a number of different brain functions. That's why there are times when researchers accidentally find that a drug developed to solve one problem has positive effects on something quite different. However, that is also why treating one part of the brain for a certain disorder may have an effect on other bodily functions. These are known as side effects. Unfortunately, some side effects can be severe enough that the person may not be able to enjoy the benefits of the drug and must stop taking it because the side effects outweigh the benefits.

If you are prescribed psychiatric medications, it is important that you follow these recommendations:

- Visit your doctor regularly. Even if you also visit other doctors, you need to keep in regular contact with the doctor who prescribed the medication. If you are given an appointment in two weeks, don't miss it. If you do not keep in touch, you are not allowing your doctor to monitor possible side effects, which may easily be controlled. You are also not allowing your doctor to monitor the effectiveness of the medication. Since there is usually more than one medication to treat any disorder, if you are not improving after a certain time limit, your doctor may prescribe a different medication.
- Let your doctor know of any changes you experience (either in your body or mind) soon after beginning to take medication. If you are feeling sick, you need to call your doctor immediately and ask whether you should stop taking the medication until she evaluates if the medication is responsible.
- Be patient. Medications may take from a few days to a few weeks before they begin to control symptoms. For example, medications for depression take at least two weeks to begin to control symptoms—and they may take as long as six weeks. Once they start to work, you'll be glad you waited.
- Take your medicine as prescribed. Some people take their depression medication only on the days they feel very depressed. This type of medication does not function like a headache remedy—you can't take it

only as needed. If you don't take the medications regularly for the prescribed time, they will not be effective. If you begin to feel better and want to stop taking your medication, you need to discuss this with the prescribing physician. Some of these medications need to be "tapered off." If they are not, you may get ill and need to go to the emergency room.

- Abstain from using drugs or alcohol. Some of these medications will make you very sick if you take them in combination with alcohol or other drugs. Others will not be as effective, and with still others your symptoms may get worse.

SIDE EFFECTS OF ANTIDEPRESSANT MEDICATIONS

Despite the years of research that went into their development, the antidepressant drugs available at this time are like crude tools for use on something as complex and delicate as the brain. Imagine that a delicate and expensive electronic device on your computer has become jammed. If you took a sledgehammer and tapped the device, you might get it to run again—but you might also damage other components in the device. The same sort of thing is true when you take a drug to cure depression. It is not surprising that there may be some bad effects along with the good effects.

It is difficult to limit the effects in the brain of a particular drug to precisely what we want to achieve; it is also very difficult to limit the effects to the brain. Drugs first go into the stomach, into muscle, or directly into the blood (if injected) and *then* into the brain. Some drugs cannot get into the brain from the blood, because of the blood-brain barrier, which helps to keep microorganisms and poisons out of the brain. For many drugs, the amount of chemical in the

Side effects such as weakness, drowsiness, and nervousness may occur when a person first begins taking an SSRI.

blood must be fairly high before it can enter the brain and be effective. This means the substance will have opportunities to act on many organs on its way to the brain.

Different antidepressants may have different side effects, and patients should always consult their physicians or pharmacists to find out exactly what to expect. However, some of the more common side effects of antidepressants include dry mouth, constipation, anxiety, heart and circulatory symptoms, and gastric upset. In a few cases, seizures have occurred. Most of the side effects are rare, and those that do occur can usually be managed, either with other medication or by adjusting dosages. The intended effects, on the other hand, may dramatically enhance a person's quality of life, making the drug worth the risks. In cases like this, side effects are a serious but usually manageable concern. However, medication should be prescribed only if the effects of the mental illness are much more serious and less manageable without medication. In other words, the disorder's risks should be more serious than the drug's. Each person should weigh the risks, benefits, and alternatives carefully with their clinician before deciding on a treatment plan.

Not everyone taking SSRI antidepressants experiences side effects, but for some people, mild side effects, such as difficulty sleeping, anxiety, weakness, tremors, sweating, *impotence*, nausea, dizziness, gastrointestinal disturbance, weight gain, drowsiness, nervousness, or yawning, may be a problem when they first take Prozac or Zoloft. In many cases, these side effects, although annoying, will go away within a few weeks and may not be serious enough to give reason to stop taking the medication. For others, the side effects can be severe and should be discussed with their medical practitioners.

Elly, for example, was having trouble sleeping because of her adjustment to a newly adopted child. She had been

> **GLOSSARY**
>
> *impotence:* The inability to have or maintain an erection.

under a lot of stress working from her home-based business, dealing with the new family member, and transporting her other children to their various functions. Her doctor suggested that she begin taking one of the SSRI antidepressants. She began with a low dose—25-milligram tablets. Her physician had her start by dividing them in half. Each week she increased by a half-tablet until she was taking the entire 25 milligrams. Once she seemed to be having no adverse effects at this dose, Elly moved in these same low increases until she was at 50 milligrams per day. Her doctor decided she should stay at this level for one month before they decided if she'd need to change her dose at her next visit.

Both Elly and her doctor were pleased with the results and neither expected what happened next. About two weeks into the month, Elly began to develop gas pains each evening. She didn't think much of it until her stools became looser and looser. By the time of her one-month visit, her stools were totally liquid and she was still experiencing quite a bit of gas pain. Elly was eating a bland diet, including chicken, turkey, rice, bread, applesauce, and bananas, but her physician felt she needed to stop taking the antidepressant. Her side effects were a problem themselves, especially since chronic diarrhea can contribute to malnutrition, which may include symptoms of depression.

Prozac, being the first of the SSRI antidepressants, has received much media attention. Sometimes, this leads to misunderstandings about drug effectiveness; advertising tends to only focus on the positive benefits of a particular drug, and consumers leap to the conclusion that it is a "miracle cure." Many times, however, a physician can find ways to help patients deal with side effects. In Elly's case, her doctor prescribed another of the SSRIs and that worked fine at a low-level dose.

Prozac has been so widely prescribed that more than 40 million people in more than ninety countries now take this

When taking medications, it is important to follow your medical practitioner's dosing instructions.

Alcohol has many effects on the mind and body. It should not be used in place of medication.

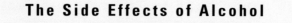

The Side Effects of Alcohol

- Alcohol is a depressant and slows down the action of the central nervous system.
- Although alcohol decreases anxiety, it is an extremely poor medication because of its serious side effects (for example, liver damage, stomach cancer, and heart disease).
- It makes one feel more relaxed, social, and talkative, but it also slows reaction time—so driving, swimming, and operating machinery become much more dangerous.
- Alcohol is addictive.
- Those who abuse alcohol may become aggressive and violent.
- Many people do things they would never do if they were not under the influence of alcohol (for example, have sex, try drugs, or commit a crime).
- Alcohol causes dehydration and may put a person at extreme risk, especially in warm weather.
- Too much alcohol can lead to unconsciousness or even death.
- Using alcohol with other depressant drugs, such as antihistamines or Valium, will increase the chance of an overdose or of vomiting while unconscious and choking to death.

medication to help them live a more effective life. The drug has undergone much safety and effectiveness study in the years since first being used to help with depression. About one in twelve patients taking Prozac develop an itching rash. This can be a serious side effect in which about one third of the persons must stop taking the drug. Other symptoms that may appear with the rash are fever, joint pain, swelling, wrist and hand pain, breathing difficulties, swollen lymph glands, and some laboratory test abnormalities. Most people have no further problems once they stop taking the drug and begin appropriate antihistamine or corticosteroid therapy.

Psychiatric Drugs Used to Treat Adjustment Disorders

	A	B	C
Class of Drugs	Heterocyclic antidepressants	Monoamine oxidase inhibitors (MAOIs)	Newer antidepressants; most are selective serotonin reuptake inhibitors (SSRIs). Some are also used in treating eating disorders.
Generic Names	clomipramine amoxapine nortriptyline amitriptyline desipramine imipramine protriptyline doxepin	isocarboxazid phenelzine tranylcypromine sulfate	fluvoxamine fluoxetine sertraline buspirone hydrochloride paroxetine venlafaxine nefazodone maprotiline
Brand Names (may be others)	Adapin Sinequan Asendin Aventyl Pamelor Elavil Endep Enovil Norpramin Pertofrane Surmontil Tofranil Janamine Vivactil	Marplan Nardil Parnate	Luvox Prozac Zoloft BusPar Paxil Effexor Serzone Ludiomil

	A	B	C
Drug Action (most likely explanation)	Block the reuptake of norepinephrine, dopamine, and serotonin; some have additional effects.	Inhibits the enzyme that breaks down norepinephrine, serotonin, and epinephrine.	Inhibit the reuptake of serotonin and/or norepinephrine.
Side Effects (partial listing)	Dry mouth (50–74%), blurred vision (6–20%), urinary retention, constipation, cardiac arrhythmias, hypertension, hypotension, or dizziness (18–52%), nausea, rash, fatigue, weight gain, sexual disturbances, increased sensitivity to sun. Most side effects disappear in a few weeks or can be managed.	Hypotension, dizziness, headache, insomnia, fatigue, tremors, and liver damage.	Usually mild; include dizziness, drowsiness, headache, nausea, difficulty with orgasm, stomach cramps, restlessness, sleeplessness, dry mouth.
Behavioral Effects if Drug Works	Mood elevation, increased physical activity, increased mental alertness, improved sleep and appetite.	Mood elevation, increased physical activity, increased mental alertness, improved sleep and appetite.	Similar to tricyclic antidepressants and MAOIs above; fluvoxamine is also used to treat obsessive-compulsive disorder.

ness of the psychiatric disorder, before making a decision, the woman should ask her clinician to help her understand the risks, benefits, and alternatives to drug treatment. Pregnancy and psychiatric drugs create an issue that needs to be thought about carefully.

Another side effect of antidepressants that is often overlooked is the withdrawal symptoms. Some of these include dizziness, stomach problems, sleep disturbances, nightmares, anxiety, irritability, numbness, or other unusual sensations. A discontinuation syndrome associated with the side effects of terminating the use of antidepressants can cause some patients to experience such distressing effects that they need to continue the drug for a longer time in an effort to slowly withdraw without the symptoms. As with anything that alters bodily functions, antidepressant use must be monitored by a physician—from beginning to end. A slow

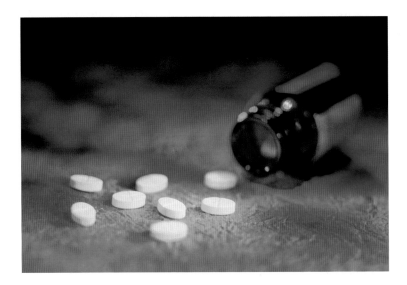

Antidepressants can cause unpleasant side effects, including unpleasant withdrawal symptoms.

A physician or other medical practitioner should always care-fully monitor the patient's entire physical condition during drug therapy.

startup and a slow discontinuation help protect patients from unnecessary problems.

Common side effects of tricyclic antidepressants include dry mouth, blurred vision, constipation, low blood pressure, and palpitations. The most common side effect is drowsiness, but about 10 to 15 percent of the patients taking it become energetic or agitated, almost to the point of hyperactivity. The way tricyclic antidepressants are metabolized within the body varies widely among patients. Tricyclic antidepressants may lose their effectiveness over time, and then the patient begins feeling the original mental issues again. In this case, the physician may give the patient some time off from the drug, after which time the effectiveness returns.

Antianxiety medication's withdrawal symptoms include poor concentration and flu-like pains.

SIDE EFFECTS OF ANTIANXIETY MEDICATIONS

Benzodiazepines can be addictive, but the addiction is usually mild, and the withdrawal effects are usually moderate and short-lived. The side effects of benzodiazepines are usually so mild that anxious patients can take therapeutic doses for years with no noticeable negative effects. However, a gradual decrease in the dosage is recommended every few months if anxiety is no longer present; that way the doctor and patient can determine whether medication is still required. Many patients fear possible side effects or social stigma caused by taking medication, and as a result, are probably more likely to take benzodiazepines for too short a time rather than too long a time. It is important to discuss risks, benefits, and alternatives with the prescribing clinician.

Even though antianxiety drugs, the benzodiazepines, are considered safe and effective for the anxiety problems associated with adjustment disorder, there is controversy over their use because of their addictive nature. Withdrawal symptoms can be a serious problem. Tapering off from low doses usually only causes sleep problems or anxiety, symptoms that may have caused the patient to take the drug initially. However, those taking a higher level of the drug—even after only four weeks of regular use—may have withdrawal symptoms that include sensitivity to bright lights, sleep disturbances, tremors, twitching, poor concentration, flu-like symptoms, and appetite loss. Those who have taken the drug for long periods of time and decide to terminate their use may experience tremors, weakness, and, most severely, *seizures*, *delirium*, depression, and even death. Before a patient changes his dose or stops taking his medication, however, he should always seek the advice of his prescribing clinician.

GLOSSARY

seizures: Convulsions caused by a sudden discharge of electrical activity in the brain.

delirium: An acute, reversible state of agitated confusion.

Barbiturates, however, are much more addictive than benzodiazepines, and overdoses are far more dangerous. Withdrawal effects are also more severe. (With any drug, withdrawal effects are more severe after a drug has been taken for a longer time and at higher doses.) Overdoses of barbiturates suppress respiration and can be fatal. Even with relatively safe benzodiazepines, as with all psychoactive drugs, great care should be taken to comply with medical advice about taking the medication, to report any side effects, and to take any recommended tests to check the physical effects of the medication.

Care must also be taken for persons suffering from severe depression, severe lung disease, sleep apnea, alcohol problems, and kidney disease. Alcohol should be avoided, along with other tranquilizers, narcotics, barbiturates, antihistamines, and antidepressants. Smoking can decrease the effectiveness of the drug.

Common side effects when taking antianxiety drugs include mild drowsiness for the first few days; sometimes the elderly become weak and confused. The side effects become more prevalent when high doses are used over long periods of time. These include headaches, irritability, confusion, memory loss, and depression.

One of the most important factors in diagnosing and treating adjustment disorders is the timing. As mentioned, these disorders are short-lived, and because they are caused by a specific stressor, once it has been eliminated, the patient will usually return to normal within six months. Treating the symptoms is important because if they are allowed to continue without relief and without training in skills like coping, relaxing, and making sound decisions, a more serious condition might develop. Such disorders might include major depression or anxiety that can persist for months or even years.

There are many different medications and many people do not get relief with the first prescription they try. Patients should be prepared to do what needs to be done and not feel discouraged if it takes some time to get relief. Other therapies may also effectively treat adjustment disorders, either alongside drug therapy or apart from it.

Monitoring one's own emotional growth and psychological progress can be an effective part of a self-help program.

7 | Alternative and Supplementary Treatments

Alternative treatments for adjustment disorder should begin with a self-help program in which the patient monitors his own behavior and learns new techniques to better deal with stress, learns healthy eating habits, and incorporates an appropriate exercise program into his routine. This should also include the approval and direction of the physician, as she can be helpful in making recommendations, observing particular health issues, and making any necessary changes in medication according to the improvement of the patient. Counseling is highly recommended for everyone diagnosed with adjustment disorder.

Therapy helps patients develop better coping skills for the future. The counselor will also help the person understand how the stressor affected her life and help her to realize solutions. Helping a client understand what has been lost and the changes this loss has caused is a big step in understanding the stressor. Choosing social and recreational activities more carefully and recommending support groups

Diet can play a role in our emotions. Some people, for example, have a sensitivity to foods like chocolate; they may crave these sweets, but when they indulge, they may feel anxious and depressed.

may be other areas where the therapist's expertise can help in the development of life skills.

Many counseling programs include help with physical strategies, such as diet and exercise. The counselor may ask the patient to do a personal assessment. What is the physical, emotional, and spiritual condition felt at that time?

DIET

The fact is that no matter what state of health a person is in, he will feel better when he eats a healthy diet. Will it be true then that someone suffering from a mood illness will feel better if he eats properly? The answer is one each individual must test. However, a healthy balance of food; no caffeine; fewer refined sugars; more fruits and vegetables; fewer processed foods; and a balance of proteins, carbohydrates, and fats will increase energy. Adding vitamins or food supplements can be useful, but it is always best to get as many vitamins and minerals from fresh food itself.

For those who have food sensitivities, being aware of and having the willpower to avoid foods that cause more symptoms can help. Someone might have a reaction to a certain food she loves, as with Deb, who loved chocolate. However, every time she ate even a small piece of chocolate, her heart raced and she felt a great surge of energy and then a terrific slump. It was worse if she ate chocolate near bedtime. When Deb was tired, it was more difficult to carry out the *cognitive* tasks she learned in therapy; therefore, she sometimes felt more anxious and depressed at night. Then, if she lay awake because of the effect of chocolate, Deb made herself more anxious by worrying. Refraining from chocolate and other caffeine products helped a great deal in her recovery.

GLOSSARY

cognitive:
Relating to or involving the elements of thought.

EXERCISE AND RELAXATION TECHNIQUES

Exercise works to keep the body in shape and to release the brain's powerful endorphins that help raise the mood level. After an appropriate exercise program, many people feel great and wonder why they had such a difficult time keeping a program regularly.

There have been recent studies that indicate that ten minutes of exercise three times a day is as productive in physical and mental health as one thirty-minute session. This is encouraging for those who feel they do not have time for a longer exercise session. One way to accomplish this task might be to park a ten-minute walk away from work or

---

Using a Journal to Cope with Adjustment Disorder with Depressed Mood

At the School of Nursing, University of Kansas Medical Center, twenty patients and their family members were taught how to monitor and cope with the depressive symptoms of adjustment disorder by keeping a daily journal. At the beginning of the sessions, the participants viewed videotaped scenes of other patients managing their own symptoms. The patients then wrote how they reacted to each scene, including what similar emotions they felt they had experienced in their own situations. When leaving, the patients were given a list of recommended activities to engage in when they were depressed. Each person was also asked to keep a daily journal for four months recording their emotions and reactions to the things they encountered in and out of their routine. They were also to rate their energy level each day. When the journals were evaluated at the end of the four-month period, the two psychiatric nurse evaluators felt the program helped influence the patients and their families to overcome many of the reactions that those who suffer from depression put themselves and their families through.

Yoga is one form of exercise that can help people better cope with the tension in their lives.

school. Then, twice in a day there would be the opportunity to exercise for ten minutes. Another time might be during a lunch or break time. Walking in place is an alternative to finding a place outside. Being creative is important when trying to make lifestyle changes.

Relaxation techniques work in the same way as exercise. Through different techniques, such as meditation, progressive body relaxation, and yoga, patients can reduce stress levels. Progressive relaxation works by teaching the patient to relax the entire body, one set of muscles at a time. Meditation works to relax the body and improve general health, even lowering blood pressure. When the mind recognizes the body during a state of relaxation, it learns how that feels and over time, it is easier and easier to get to that state when in a stressful situation. Sometimes a key word or phrase is practiced while relaxing, and that word can be a relaxation trigger during a stressful time at work or school.

Education can help us learn more effective ways for coping with the "dragons" we all face.

EDUCATION

Learning about mood disorders such as adjustment disorder by reading, asking doctors questions, and joining a support group, helps the patient feel a part of the treatment plan. Being ***proactive*** helps the patient feel able to manage current issues, as well as keeps him from fearing the future. The medical world, both physical and psychological, is constantly changing—what is a problem today may have a solution tomorrow. Making certain that the immediate physical problems are under control is the first step. However, understanding mental issues as well is essential to keeping the patient willing and able to care for himself in the best possible manner.

Meditation techniques can be practiced anywhere.

Saint-John's-wort has been used for centuries to treat both mental and physical disorders.

NATURAL REMEDIES

Although psychiatric drugs can effectively treat the depression and anxiety of an adjustment disorder, medication is not an option for some individuals. These people may feel more comfortable using herbal or other natural alternatives. These natural alternatives include herbs such as ginseng, Saint-John's-wort, kava, and valerian.

Although not approved in the United States for medicinal treatment, ginseng root has been used in Chinese medicine for centuries. Supporters of herbal therapy believe ginseng has many beneficial effects: it boosts the immune system, increases energy levels, aids in stress management, and reduces depressive symptoms. Ginseng is widely available in numerous forms, including tea, pill, and extract form.

Saint-John's-wort has been used for hundreds of years in Greece, China, Europe, and North America for treating both physical and mental illnesses. European studies found Saint-John's-wort to be very effective in treating depression and anxiety, but the U.S. Food and Drug Administration has not approved it for such treatments. It can be purchased over the counter in health food, grocery, and drug stores.

Kava, a member of the pepper family that grows in the South Pacific Islands, is another herb that has been used to treat depression and anxiety. Kava root seems to have a calming effect on the mind, and it is also used as a muscle relaxant. European studies indicate that kava root has the beneficial properties of benzodiazepines without the negative side effects. In very high doses, however, kava may have side effects of its own, including sleepiness and skin irritation. It can be purchased over the counter but has not been approved for medicinal use by the U.S. Food and Drug Administration.

Plant Extracts That Treat the Mind

A study of outpatients diagnosed with adjustment disorder with a subcategory of anxiety was coordinated by a group of psychiatrists using Euphtose (EUP). EUP is a combination of six plant extracts, including crataegus, ballota, passiflora, and valerian, which have mild sedative effects, and cola and paullina, which mainly act as mild stimulants. The participants included ninety-one patients from the EUP group and ninety-one persons from the placebo group.

Each person received two tablets three times per day for twenty-eight days. They were then evaluated using the Hamilton-anxiety rating scale on the day before they began the medication and on days seven, fourteen, and twenty-eight. When the two groups were compared, 42.9 percent of the EUP group had an anxiety rating score of less than ten on day twenty-eight, while only 25.3 percent of the placebo group scored in the same range. The anxiety rating score for the EUP group decreased from 26.16 on day zero to 19.65 on day seven, 15.36 on day fourteen, and down to 12.63 on day twenty-eight, while the placebo group went from 21.37 on day zero to 15.2 on day twenty-eight. Thus, these results showed that for those suffering with adjustment disorder with anxiety, EUP worked better than the placebo.

Valerian is another herb that has been around for centuries; it is used both as a sleep aid and as a temporary remedy for anxiety. It seems to act as a sedative, but as with most herbal remedies, it is not approved by the U.S. Food and Drug Administration for medicinal use.

Even though they are natural remedies, herbs can still have powerful effects on the body and can interact with other medications. Just because a remedy is labeled "natural" or "herbal" does not mean that it is always safe or that it won't have any side effects. Since the U.S. Food and Drug Administration has not approved these substances for medicinal use, these substances are not subject to the same rigorous quality controls that apply to approved drugs. Even if the herb itself is safe for ingestion, there is no guarantee that the herb has been manufactured in a pure or safe way.

An old proverb says, "He who treats himself has a fool for a doctor." People using natural remedies should always ask their doctor about them.

HOW FRIENDS AND FAMILY MEMBERS CAN HELP PEOPLE WITH ADJUSTMENT DISORDERS

Relationships play an important part in the recovery of a person with an adjustment disorder. A study performed in London with depressed people (reported in the *British Journal of Psychiatry*) found that depressed people who received

---

Homeopathic Treatment for Adjustment Disorders

Homeopathy is a form of alternative medicine that treats disease and disorders from a very different perspective from conventional medicine. It looks at a person's entire physical and mental being, rather than dividing a patient into various symptoms and disorders. Homeopathic medicine uses tiny doses to stimulate the body's ability to heal itself. In some cases, these doses may be administered only once every few months or years.

According to Judyth Reichenberg-Ullman and Robert Ullman, authors of *Prozac Free: Homeopathic Medicine for Depression, Anxiety, and Other Mental and Emotional Problems*, homeopathy offers safe, natural alternatives that can supplement or replace conventional pharmaceutical treatment. They recommend this form of treatment because it has fewer side effects than conventional drugs. Homeopathic treatment should always be administered by a licensed homeopathic practitioner.

no drug therapy but did receive psychotherapy for both themselves and their partners recovered more quickly than those who received only drugs. Support from others is an important element of recovery for those suffering from an adjustment disorder.

If someone you know has an adjustment problem, one of the first things you can do to help is to become informed. You might want to read a book written by a person with an adjustment disorder. Usually, it is hard for someone in the midst of an adjustment problem to explain what she is feeling. Someone else's words may help you to understand— and if you can understand, you can be a better support for your family member or friend. Or you may want to read a book written by a professional that provides information on

All of us face many tensions in life.

When a person is experiencing an adjustment disorder, it causes strain in his relationships with others.

adjustment disorders so that you can understand the disease better and know what to expect in the future.

Forgiveness also plays an important part in helping family members who are coping with an adjustment disorder. Remember that the disorder causes changes in behavior; the people you care about may not be able to carry out their regular daily tasks. They sometimes cannot care for themselves, let alone others. This may make you feel abandoned and left out. It's okay to be upset—but blame the *disorder*, not the *person* you love.

If someone in your family is experiencing an adjustment disorder, be sure to take care of yourself. Adjustment disorders can cause pain and stress in the lives of the entire family. Try to minimize its effect on you by practicing good

Someone who has experienced a major life loss needs support and encouragement from those around him.

In his book *Life After Loss,* Bob Deits suggests that when responding to losses or changes in life, following these suggestions might help you get back on track:

- Identify exactly what it is you have lost. Make sure that when you lose money in a deal, it is the money that is the loss, rather than your self-esteem.
- Do a personal assessment of your physical, intellectual, and spiritual condition.
- Talk about your loss and the grief you feel because of it. Try to keep a journal as well as tell others how you feel.
- Find a support community either at your place of worship, or support group.

health habits yourself. If you stay well, you will be better able to support your family member or friend.

Sometimes the best thing you can do to help someone with an adjustment disorder is to just listen. By listening, you can better understand what your family member's needs are. People with mental health disorders need to talk about their feelings. Be understanding and encourage your family member (or friend) to share with you, to learn about his condition, and to seek help. Be particularly sensitive to any threats of suicide. People with mental health disorders may feel that suicide is the only way out of their pain. Attempts are usually preceded by threats, even if they are mild. Don't ignore any comments about death. Ask the person whether they are contemplating suicide. If you think they are in danger, call a doctor.

You may need to be a caregiver at times. Sometimes adjustment disorders can cause memory impairment and problems with concentration. This may be a function of the disorder or of the stress associated with having the disorder. Remind your family member to take her medication, to go to appointments; help her with her chores. The person you love is not ignoring her responsibilities—she is merely unable to function normally because of the disorder.

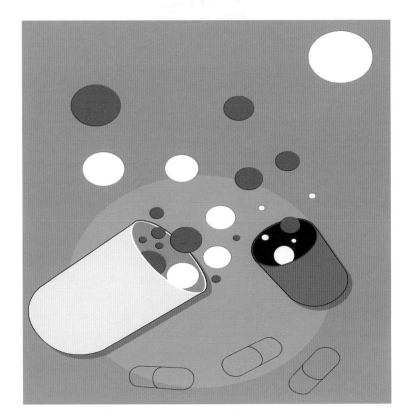

Psychiatric drugs can play an important role in therapy for a person with an adjustment disorder—but medication is not the only answer.

Try to accept the reality of the adjustment disorder that is affecting your family's life. If you are having difficulty accepting the fact that your loved one has a mental health disorder, you will only make it more difficult for that person to accept it as well. If you do not acknowledge the disorder, you may react with anger, instead of with sympathy, to the person's behavior; your friend or family member needs your understanding and compassion. Talk to other family members, even young children. Together, you can help each other understand what the condition is and what it means for your life as a family. You may want to join a support group or ask the patient's therapist for a few sessions of family therapy. Any of these can help you learn to deal with the adjustment disorder.

If you know someone with an adjustment disorder, remember that person is suffering from an illness. It won't just go away when someone wants it to or when it is becoming a nuisance. As with any sickness, it requires medical attention and attention from family members.

SUMMARY

Psychiatric drugs often play an important role in helping people with an adjustment disorder. However, drugs are far from being the only answer. Research shows that medication combined with psychotherapy works best, but in many cases, time alone brings strength and healing to those struggling to adjust to a new reality in their lives. There is no need to suffer needlessly, though, simply to prove one's strength. Both alternative treatments and drug therapy, whether used alone or combined, offer real help to those suffering from an adjustment disorder.

FURTHER READING

Bridges, William. *Transitions.* Reading, Mass.: Perseus Books, 1990.

Clayton, Lawrence. *Tranquilizers.* Springfield, N.J.: Enslow, 1997.

Deits, Bob. *Life after Loss.* Tucson, Ariz.: Fisher Books, 1998.

Monroe, Judy. *Antidepressants.* Springfield, N.J.: Enslow, 1997.

Wilens, Timothy E. *Straight Talk About Psychiatric Medications for Kids.* New York: The Guilford Press, 2001.

Witkin, Georgia. *KidStress: What It Is, How It Feels, How to Help.* New York: Viking Penguin, 1999.

FOR MORE INFORMATION

American Academy of Child and Adolescent Psychiatry
3615 Wisconsin Avenue, NW
Washington, DC 20016-3007
www.aacap.org

American Academy of Pediatrics
601 Thirteenth Street, NW
Suite 400, North
Washington, DC 20005
800-336-5475
www.aap.org

Child & Family Canada
www.cfc-efc.ca/index.shtml

Federation of Families for Children's Mental Health
1101 King Street
Suite 420
Alexandria, VA 22314
703-648-7710
www.ffcmh.org

Internet Mental Health
www.mentalhealth.com/p.html

National Institute of Mental Health
NMH Public Inquires
6001 Executive Blvd.
Rm. 8184, MSC 9663
Bethesda, MD 20892-9663

Psych Central: Adjustment Disorders
psychcentral.com/disorders/sx6t.htm

Publisher's Note:

The Web sites listed on this page were active at the time of publication. The publisher is not responsible for Web sites that have changed their address or discontinued operation since the date of publication. The publisher will review and update the Web sites upon each reprint.

INDEX

BIOGRAPHIES

Sherry Bonnice lives with her husband and two children on a dirt road in rural Pennsylvania. They raise rabbits and have a small farm with a goat, a sheep, chickens, one duck, five dogs, and two cats. Sherry has spent the last two years coediting three quilt magazines and writing a quilt book. She has also written several books for other Mason Crest series, including Careers with Character and North American Folklore.

Mary Ann Johnson is a licensed child and adolescent clinical nurse specialist and a family psychiatric nurse practitioner in the state of Massachusetts. She completed her psychotherapy training at Cambridge Hospital and her psychopharmacology training at Massachusetts General Hospital. She is the director of clinical trials in the pediatric psychopharmacology research unit at Massachusetts General Hospital and she has her own private practice as well.

Donald Esherick has spent seventeen years working in the pharmaceutical industry and is currently an associate director of Worldwide Regulatory Affairs with Wyeth Research in Philadelphia, Pennsylvania. He specializes in the chemistry section (manufacture and testing) of investigational and marketed drugs.